Greenwich
and
the London River

Paul Tempest

drawings by Peter Kent

photographs by Stephen Tempest

Medina Publishing

Greenwich and the London River

Medina Publishing Ltd
83 Ewell Road
Surbiton
Surrey KT6 6AH

www.medinapublishing.com

IBSN: 978-0-9567081-9-9

1 3 5 7 9 0 8 6 4 2

Drawings by Peter Kent
Photographs by Stephen Tempest
Cartoons by Clare Tempest; sailing memories by Susie Tempest
Designed by Sam Elverson
Edited by Peter Harrigan
Printed and bound by Short Run Press Ltd, Exeter

CIP Data: A catalogue record for this book is available from the British Library.

Contents

Road, Rail and River – the London Commuters

The Daily Commuters of London Bridge
Boris Johnson

Still they come, surging towards me across the bridge.

   On they march in sun, wind rain, snow and sleet.
Almost every morning I cycle past them in rank after
heaving rank as they emerge from London Bridge
station and tramp tramp tramp up and along the broad
239-metre pavement that leads over the river and towards their places of
work...

   ...Sometimes they are on the phone, or talking to their neighbours, or
checking their texts. A few of them may glance at the scene, which is
certainly worth a glance: on their left the glistening turrets of the City, on
the right the white Norman keep, the guns of HMS *Belfast* and the mad
castellations of Tower Bridge, and beneath them the powerful swirling
eddies of the river that seems to be green or brown depending on the
time of day. Mainly, however, they have their mouths set and eyes with that
blank and inward look of people who have done the bus or the Tube or the

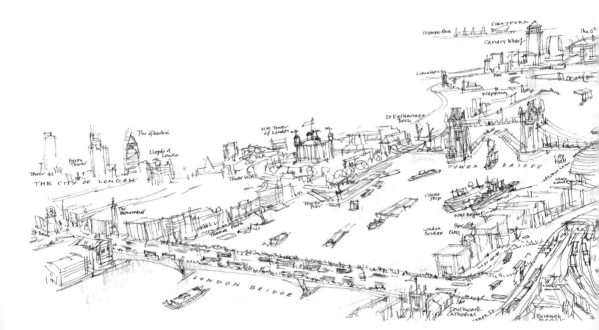

overground train and are steeling themselves for the day ahead...

...By the time I get to cycle home, most of the morning crowds have tramped the other way. Like some gigantic undersea coelenterate, London has completed its spectacularly daily act of respiration – sucking in millions of commuters from 7 am to 9 am, and then efficiently expelling them back to the suburbs and Home Counties from 5 pm to 7 pm. But the drift home is more staggered. There are pubs, clubs and bars to be visited and as I watch the crowds of drinkers on the pavements – knots of people dissolving and reforming in a slow minuet – I can see why the city beats the countryside hands down. It's the sheer range of opportunity...

City Hall, on the South Bank close to Tower Bridge and east of HMS *Belfast*.

...The metropolis is like a vast multinational reactor where Mr Quark and Miss Neutrino are moving the fastest and bumping into each other with the most exciting results. This is not just a question of romance and reproduction. It is about ideas. It is about the cross-pollination that is more likely to take place with a whole superswarm of bees rather than a few isolated hives.

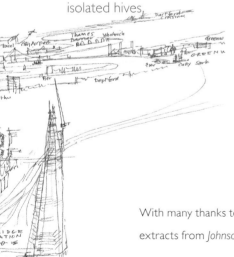

With many thanks to Boris Johnson for his permission to quote these extracts from *Johnson's Life of London* published by Harper Press in 2011

With that I saw two swans of goodly hue,

Come softly swimming down along the Lee...

So purely white they were,

That even the gentle stream, the which them bare

Seemed foul to them, and bade his billows spare

To wet their silken feathers, lest they might

Soil their fair plumes with water not so fair

And mar their beauties bright,

That shone as Heaven's light,

Against their bridal day, which was not long:

Sweet Thames, run softly, till I end my song.

from *Prothalamion* (1596) by Edmund Spenser (1552-99)

Wake Up, London!

For Londoners on both North and South Banks, the water of our sweet River Thames literally flows through us daily. Also, twice a day, its fierce salty tides sweep in and out of the capital, linking the metropolis constantly to the unpredictability of the estuary, sea and ocean. Today, we tend to take the London River for granted, forgetting that long-term neglect would spell disaster and chaos.

On the southern shore lies a very special jewel – Greenwich. Here, marked by the Meridian line of the Royal Observatory on the crest of the hill, is man's agreed base-point for the measurement of time and space. Below is the great horseshoe curve of the River round the Isle of Dogs and the new high-rise offices of Canary Wharf. In the foreground are the gleaming masterpiece buildings of Christopher Wren and John Vanbrugh and the tall masts of the newly-restored *Cutty Sark*. Beyond and clearly visible to the left, are the dome of St Paul's Cathedral and the new high Shard at London Bridge. To the right lies the white roof of the O_2 Arena, and not far beyond, across the River, the 2012 Olympic stadium and village.

Here, close neighbours in Greenwich, Peter Kent and I have lived happily for over 50 years, participating in, writing about and illustrating its daily life and that of the rapidly-changing River. My son, Stephen, has been photographing its treasures and people and visitors for half that period, publishing guidebooks at ten-year intervals and working for ten years in the National Maritime Museum. For all three of us, this book is not so much a formal guidebook as a drawing together of disparate threads, an expression of affection and love to mark the important role of Greenwich and Woolwich in the 2012 London Olympics.

Finally, I offer my own personal assessment of how the London River has changed over the last forty years, and what might lie in store over the next forty.

Paul Tempest, April 2012

The river sweats

Oil and tar

The barges drift

With the turning tide

Red sails

Wide

To leeward, swing on the heavy spar.

The barges wash

Drifting logs

Down Greenwich reach

Past the Isle of Dogs ...

from *The Waste Land: Section III The Fire Sermon* (1922)
by TS Eliot (1888-1965)

The Millennium Dome looking across Canary Wharf upstream to Tower Bridge

CONGRATULATIONS!

Queen's

Diamond Jubilee

Welcome to

WE · GOVERN · BY · SERVING

ROYAL *borough of*
GREENWICH

Royal Greenwich and the Diamond Jubilee

Royal Greenwich and the 2012 Diamond Jubilee

A succession of major events has been planned in 2012 to mark the 60th Anniversary of the reign of HM the Queen

The Royal Borough

The Letter Patent, formally confirming the granting of the status of Greenwich as a Royal Borough, was presented to Greenwich on 3 February

2012, with special events and fireworks on 4 and 5 February on Greenwich Riverside and in Eltham Town Centre. The new coat of arms of the Royal Borough of Greenwich was designed by the Royal College of Arms and is now displayed and used throughout the Borough.

The Re-opening of the Cutty Sark

The re-opening of the restored 19th century clipper Cutty Sark in the presence of HM the Queen and the Duke of Edinburgh took place on

25 April 2012. Built in 1869 for £16,500, the restoration cost more than £50 million. Since the devastating fire in 2007, the midships have been rebuilt and the whole ship raised in its dry dock to provide new conference and exhibition spaces, and refreshment facilities for the public beneath the hull.

The Royal River Exhibition

On 27 April a major exhibition titled *Royal River: Power and Pageantry and the Thames* will open in the new Sammy Ofer Wing of the National Maritime Museum, which in 2012 will be celebrating its 75th anniversary. HM the Queen, as Princess Elizabeth, attended the inaugural ceremony with her parents on 27 April 1937. Prince Philip, Duke of Edinburgh, has been a Trustee and Patron of the Museum for the last 63 years. Highlights of the Exhibition (which will close on 9 September 2012) include 49 items from the Royal Collection, many on display for the first time; 250 items on loan from other museums and galleries round the world; and a display of major artworks by Canaletto. Visitors will be able to view the stern carvings of the Royal Yacht *Victoria and Albert III* and Handel's autographed score of the Music for the Royal Fireworks.

The Thames Royal Pageant

The Thames Diamond Jubilee Royal Pageant will be held on Sunday 3 June, with a procession of 1,000 boats, an anticipated 30,000 people afloat and close to a million spectators on the banks. The procession flotilla will stretch for seven miles and take an hour and a half to pass. The Queen's Barge, the *Spirit of Chartwell,* a Pullman-like launch stripped of its masts and fitted out in red and gold to look like an 18th century Royal barge, will be accompanied by the Royal Row-Barge *Gloriana*, an 88ft gilded barge rowed by 18 oarsmen.

Other vessels include three-master sail training vessels, a flotilla of Little Ships that took part in the evacuation from Dunkirk in 1940, canal narrow-boats, various Dutch sailing barges, Essex oyster smacks, Chinese dragon boats, Australian surf and outrigger fishing boats from New Zealand and, it is rumoured, the Mayor of London in a Welsh coracle. Modelled on the pageants for Queen Ann Boleyn's coronation in 1533, for King Charles II in 1662 and for King George I in 1716, music will be provided by bands and orchestras afloat and ashore, the pealing of bells by the City churches and fanfares of trumpeters on each of the bridges. The Queen will take the salute near Tower Bridge and many of the vessels will continue downriver to Greenwich. This spectacular exhibition is guest-curated by historian David Starkey and includes one of the largest-ever loans of Royal Collection objects to any museum.

Sail Royal Greenwich

About 20 square-rigged sail training vessels will be moored in the Woolwich Reach for the period of the 2012 London Olympic Games, from Wednesday 25 July to Sunday 12 August 2012. Access will be from the Royal Arsenal Pier at Woolwich Dockyard. Each afternoon and evening, a group of them will sail upriver to Tower Bridge and back to Woolwich. Large visiting motor yachts will be accommodated in the Millwall Dock reached through the West India Dock Entrance opposite the 0_2 Arena.

Above: the tallship *Thalassa* is being used to train captains in the specifics of piloting the tidal Thames in preparation for the Sail Royal Greenwich event.

Royal Connections with Greenwich

1082   In the name of the King, the land round Greenwich held by Bishop Odo of Bayeux and given to him by his half-brother William the Conqueror is seized and declared the property of present and future Kings.

1300   King Edward III establishes a Royal Hunting Lodge. Monarchs become regular visitors.

1415   King Henry V is met by the Lord Mayor of London on Blackheath on the return of the Army from victory over the French at Agincourt.

1428   After the death of Henry V in 1422, his half-brother Humphrey of Gloucester acting as regent builds Bella Court, a new palace in Greenwich for King Henry VI.

1431   King Henry VI returns from his coronation in Paris as King of France to a tumultuous welcome on Blackheath.

1447   Duke Humphrey is arrested for treason and Bella Court is claimed by Queen Margaret of Anjou, the consort of Henry VI, who renames it The Palace of Placentia ("the pleasant palace").

1491   Henry Tudor is born in Greenwich and baptised in St Alfege's Church.

1502   Henry becomes heir to the throne on the death of his brother Arthur, and in 1509 marries Catherine of Aragon in the Palace of Placentia. A daughter, Mary, is born.

1533   Henry's second wife, Ann Boleyn, is crowned Queen by the Lord Mayor of London in Greenwich and gives birth to a daughter, Elizabeth at the Palace of Placentia.

1536   Ann Boleyn is arrested in Greenwich after King Henry VIII suspects adultery, and he has her beheaded.

1540   Ann of Cleves, betrothed to Henry, meets him on Blackheath and is escorted by large crowds to Greenwich where they embark for their wedding in Westminster.

1547   Henry VIII dies and in 1553 his son Edward, aged 15, dies suddenly at the Palace of Placentia of suspected poisoning. Lady Jane Grey is named as his successor, but within 9 days she is charged with murder, de-throned and beheaded.

Edward's sister, Mary becomes Queen. Elizabeth is crowned Queen Elizabeth I at age 25 and makes Placentia her main place of residence, where in 1587 she signs Mary's death-warrant.

1603   Queen Elizabeth I dies of suspected blood-poisoning, to be succeeded by King James I (King James VI of Scotland) who in 1614 gives the Greenwich Palace of Placentia to his wife, Queen Ann of Denmark. She immediately commissions the construction of a new building in the Palladian style; this is the Queen's House that stands more or less unchanged to this day.

1625   King Charles I rules from Greenwich on the death of his father, James I. Civil War breaks out and Charles I is captured and beheaded in Whitehall. From 1652 the Palace is used as a residence by the "usurper". Cromwell and other areas are developed as a Prisoner of War camp for Dutch prisoners and a large biscuit factory.

1660   Charles II is welcomed home on Blackheath, and in Greenwich he orders the pulling down of the Palace of Placentia to make way for a new building to be designed by Christopher Wren and to be used as a Royal Naval Hospital for Seamen.

1675   Greenwich Royal Observatory is commissioned by Royal Warrant.

1751   The Royal Naval Hospital is completed and by 1814 houses more than 2500 veterans. It closes in 1869 to become the Royal Naval College, dedicated to training the officers of the Royal Navy and remains in this capacity for another 125 years. It is then handed over to the new University of Greenwich.

1947   Lieutenant Philip Mountbatten is made Baron Greenwich on the morning of his wedding to Princess Elizabeth, now Queen Elizabeth II.

2012   Queen Elizabeth II, in the year of her Diamond Jubilee, makes Greenwich a Royal Borough, the fourth to be so honoured.

The Four Royal Boroughs

Greenwich:
granted Royal status in 2012

Windsor and Maidenhead:
granted Royal status in 1974

Kensington and Chelsea:
granted Royal status in 1965

Kingston upon Thames:
granted Royal status in 1965

From top: the Queen's House and the National Maritime Museum, with the Canary Wharf complex in the distance.

Rowers on Dorney Lake, the venue for the Olympic rowing, flatwater canoeing and Paralympic rowing events, with Windsor Castle in the background.

The Albert Memorial in Kensington Gardens, and the Albert Hall in the background.

Kingston Bridge looking towards Teddington.

Citius, altius, fortius

Motto of the Olympic Games

Make Britain Proud
Back the Bid

Olympic and Paralympic Greenwich

Olympics 2012

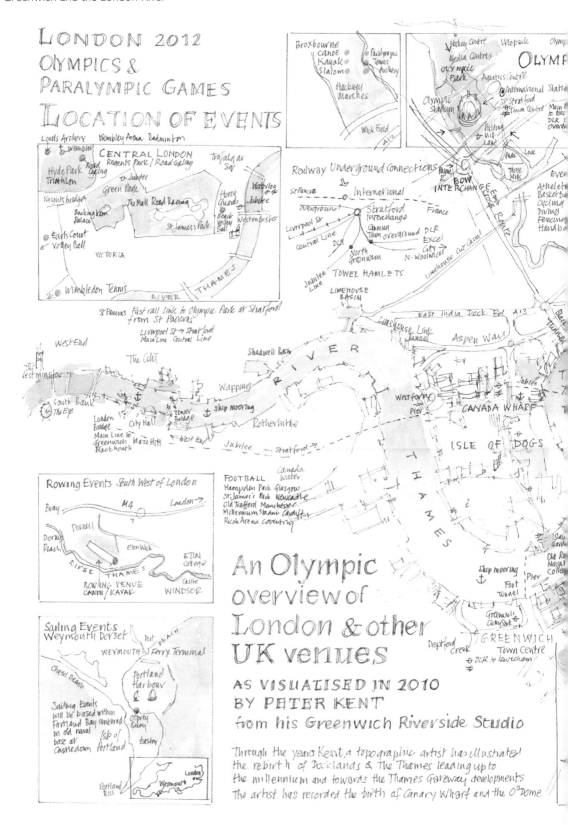

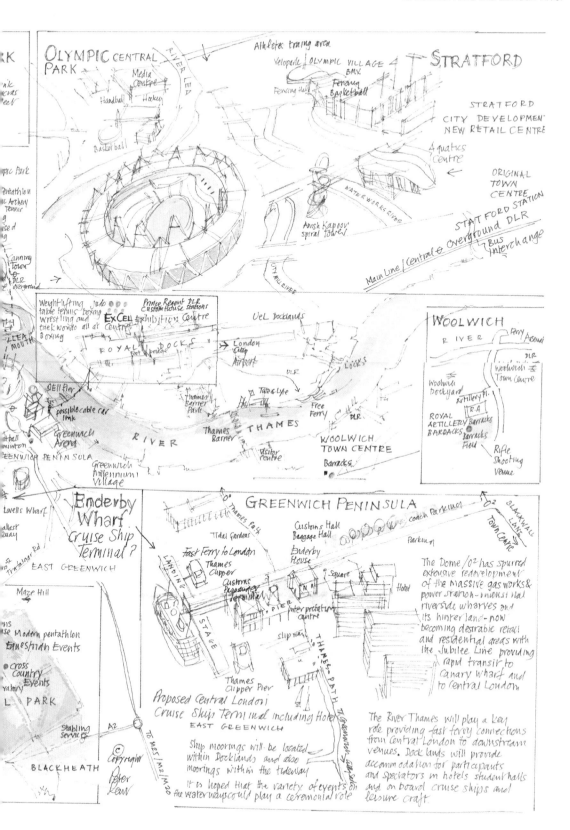

The 2012 London Olympic Games

Venues beside or close to the London River

Greenwich Park will host the Olympic and Paralympic Equestrian competitions. There will be 19 events devoted to Jumping, Dressage, Eventing and Paralympic Equestrian. A temporary Cross-Country course is being constructed in the upper part of the Park, while a temporary main arena area will be provided in front of the National Maritime Museum. In addition the Modern Pentathlon will be held in the Park as a combined running and shooting event.

North Greenwich Arena and the **O₂ Arena**, located on the Greenwich Peninsula close to North Greenwich station on the Jubilee Line, will host Artistic Gymnastics, Trampoline, Basketball and Wheelchair Basketball. There will be 20 events.

The Royal Artillery Barracks at Woolwich on the edge of Woolwich Common will host the Shooting events, Paralympic Shooting and Paralympic Archery events. Olympic Archery will take place at Lords Cricket Ground at St John's Wood close to Regent Park.

Hadleigh Farm, near Lee-on-See, Essex, overlooking the marshes and the estuary on the North Bank of the Thames, will host the Mountain Bike events.

The Olympic Stadium in the south of the **Olympic Park** at Stratford has a seating capacity of 80,000. There will be 208 events.

The Basketball Arena is located in the north of the **Olympic Park**. It will host Basketball, Wheelchair Basketball, Wheelchair Rugby and the final stage of a Handball Competition. There will be seven events.

The Aquatics Centre is part of the gateway to the **Olympic Park**. It will host Diving, Swimming, Synchronised Swimming, Paralympic Swimming and the Modern Pentathlon. There will be 192 events.

The BMX Track is in the north part of the **Olympic Park**. It will host two events of BMX Cycling.

From top: the new Olympic Shooting venue near the Royal Artillery Barracks at Woolwich was designed by Magma Architecture. The temporary, reusable structure is clad in around 18,000 sqm of PVC membrane. It has been nicknamed 'the octopus' – for obvious reasons.

The Velodrome is the most sustainable venue in the Olympic Park in terms of design and construction. It makes optimal use of natural light, reducing the need for electric lighting.

The unique design of the Basketball Arena is captured by a sunset in August 2011. Like the shooting venue, it will be dismantled after the Games.

The Copper Box is in the west of the **Olympic Park**. It will be the venue for Handball, Goalball, and the Fencing discipline of the Modern Pentathlon. There will be six events.

The Riverbank Arena will host Hockey, Paralympic Five-a-side Football and Seven-a-side Football. There will be four events.

ExCeL, the exhibition and conference centre alongside the Royal Victoria Dock on the North Bank will host (in five separate arenas) Boxing, Fencing, Judo, Table Tennis, Paralympic Judo, Paralympic Powerlifting, Sitting Volleyball and Wheelchair Fencing. There will be 165 events.

The Mall, London SW1, with Buckingham Palace at one end and Trafalgar Square at the other, will provide the start and finish of the Olympic and Paralympic Marathons and the Olympic Cycling Road Races. There will be 11 events.

Wheelchair Rugby

From top:

Back the Bid campaign poster: Make Britain Proud.

The Olympic stadium viewed from Old Ford Lock on the River Lee Navigation at the start of the Hackney Cut.

The O_2 Arena looking looking south from Greenwich. Because of Olympic sponsorship rules, the venue will be known for the duration of the Games as the North Greenwich Arena.

The view of the Olympic stadium as seen from the Olympic Park explains why it has been likened to a flying saucer.

Left: one of the Royal Mail's series of London 2012 Olympic Games stamps, this one featuring Wheelchair Rugby, which will take place at the Basketball Arena.

Above: artist's impression of the Equestrian arena in Greenwich Park for the 2012 Olympics.

Below: artist's impression of the Aquatics Centre at the south-east corner of the Olympic Park.

Above: with the Velodrome in the background, two keen BMX riders try out the new track. The Shard at London Bridge is just visible on the left skyline.

If you seek my monument, look around you!

Christopher Wren

2000
Years
of
History

Two Thousand Years in Greenwich History

70   Approximate earliest date of the Roman Temple in Greenwich Park.

650   Approximate date of the 20 Saxon burial mounds in Greenwich Park.

1012   The Vikings murder Alfege, Archbishop of Canterbury at Greenwich.

1390   Geoffrey Chaucer, author of *The Canterbury Tales* is appointed Royal Commissioner for the River between Greenwich and Woolwich.

1509   Henry VIII is pronounced King. He spent much time supervising the Royal Dockyards of Deptford and Woolwich from the Royal Palace of Placentia at Greenwich.

1614   Construction of the Queen's House begins for Queen Anne of Denmark, wife of King James I.

1675   John Flamsteed is appointed first Astronomer Royal and housed in the new Royal Observatory designed by Sir Christopher Wren.

1694   Sir Christopher Wren begins work on the new Seamen's Hospital, completed by Nicholas Hawksmoor and John Vanbrugh and occupied until the end of 1998 by the Royal Naval College.

1759   General James Wolfe leaves the family home, McCartney House in Greenwich, for Quebec, where he dies. His body is returned to be buried in St. Alfege's, Greenwich.

1775   Captain James Cook RN is appointed a Captain of the Royal Hospital at Greenwich after completion of his second voyage of discovery in the Pacific Ocean.

1805   Horatio Nelson (born 1758, later Viscount Nelson) lies in state in the Painted Hall following his death at the Battle of Trafalgar on 21 October1805.

1815   Regular passenger services by steamboat are inaugurated between London, Greenwich and Gravesend.

1838   The London-Greenwich steam railway opens.

1866 Brunel's *Great Eastern*, built on the Isle of Dogs, successfully completes the laying of the Atlantic telegraph cable, manufactured and loaded in East Greenwich. At her launch she was by far the largest ship in the world.

1884 Greenwich as the global prime meridian is confirmed at a conference in Washington DC, USA.

1905 Start of the Penny Steamer commuter services on the Thames.

1954 The tea-clipper *Cutty Sark* arrives at her present dry-dock berth.

1972 LORICA, the London River Commuters Association, is founded in Greenwich. First hydrofoil and hovercraft services run between 1972 and 1976.

1999 Greenwich Millennium Dome opened. The Docklands Light Railway and Jubilee lines are extended to Greenwich. The Royal Naval College is handed over to the University of Greenwich. New river commuter service promised.

2005 Extensive fast passenger services introduced between Westminster, Greenwich and Woolwich.

2012 Greenwich granted Royal Borough status.
The London Olympic Games held.

Right: the 18th century Coade stone lion was made by Benjamin West as a trial piece for the pediment in the King William Courtyard to commemorate Admiral Nelson. It is now in the Discover Greenwich exhibition.

Past Travellers to Greenwich

For the Romans established in Londinium two thousand years ago, it was the first hill downstream, beyond the marsh – and the point, on that bleak heath above the green woods, where the imperial highway swung away from the River and across the rolling hills of Kent to Dover and the Channel.

For later travellers, the five miles of River with its swift tides competed strongly with the road. The crest of the hill above Greenwich was the point where Crusaders, pilgrims to Canterbury and countless other venturers looked back for their last sight of the spires and ramparts of London. Equally, it was the point where ambassadors from the continent and other travellers paused with, suddenly, the capital at their feet. Here, rebel armies, such as those of Wat Tyler mustered, and countless military reviews and public demonstrations took place. Meanwhile, the town by the River prospered; the Royal Dockyards, founded close by at Deptford by Henry VIII, and the vast expansion of port facilities brought other trade and industry and many more people to the River. It is not surprising that the people of London streamed out on high-days and holidays to the great fairs at Greenwich, Blackheath and Charlton and came down the River to see the endless procession of ships or simply to smell the sweet country air.

In the 17th and 18th centuries the hostelries and entertainments of Greenwich had multiplied and catered for many tastes. The citizens of London came to frolic, to escape the plague. Or else they sent their wives for the summer. As one writer of 1700 put it 'there is in Greenwich no manner of Dainties to incline them to extravagance'. The twice-yearly horse and cattle fairs on the Heath grew into major public entertainments. Like Samuel Pepys, many came to Greenwich often to detach themselves from from the narrow tumult of everyday city life and ponder upon wider issues.

The 19th century brought day-trippers by paddle steamer, on what the *Times* called London's fairy stream; and also, from 1838, by railway. They ate Greenwich whitebait, drank porter and swipes in the many taverns, played kiss-in-the-ring in the park, tumbled hand-in-hand down One Tree Hill and

were locked for misdemeanors in the 12th century hollow oak, which is still there. They patronised the music halls, toured the limestone Hellfire Caverns under Point Hill and continued to frequent circuses, fairs and shows. Although the great Spring Fair, which Charles Dickens described as '*a three-day fever which cools the blood for six months*', was suppressed in 1859 on account of hooliganism and the Caverns closed after a notorious masked ball, Greenwich retained its popularity.

Although the Royal imprint was now faint and the Royal Hunt had moved elsewhere, the gentlemen of the area still kept large stables. Golf, first played on Blackheath by James I in about 1608, was pursued with vigour. Rugby, football, ballooning and cricket were also being enjoyed. Above all Greenwich Park was still a place for lovers, with its enchanting hillocks and arbours, its quiet glades and walks and its splendid views. As the *Comic Guide to Greenwich* put it '*the Park was where the soldiers caught the nursemaids and the children caught the cold*'.

The 20th century brought electric trams to Greenwich; for a short time, a Penny Steamer service, but gradually also fewer trains, slower buses and little relief for the private car. Even more industry and suburban sprawl swallowed up almost every patch of green apart from the Heath and the Park. After 1945 on the River, the crumbling wharves and empty docks were gradually abandoned; many of the bombed sites sprouted weed and verdure, untouched.

Here is the graveyard of many brave words, bold promises, fine projects. But wait before you draw conclusions.

Stand across the River in Island Gardens and see the same view which Canaletto painted about 1752 (see next page). This view of Greenwich Hospital may have been commissioned by Consul Joseph Smith for his residence on the Grand Canal. He was British Consul in Venice from 1744 to 1760, where he entertained many English Grand Tourists. Canaletto worked in England from 1746 to late 1755. This view was probably begun in 1752, perhaps to mark the Hospital's completion in the previous year.

A view of Greenwich Hospital by Canaletto c.1755.

Views from the past: 1814

Rough water: west wind against incoming tide at Greenwich.
Greenwich from the River, showing the Royal Naval College.
Engraving by A W B Cooke

1972 to 1975

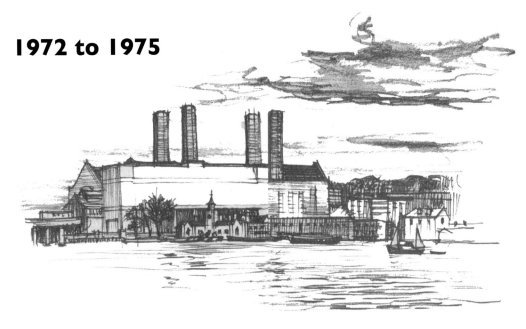

Dating from 1616, Trinity Hospital is the oldest surviving building in
Greenwich town centre and is seen here dwarfed by Greenwich Power
Station, which was completed in 1910.

The view downriver from Greenwich in 1975 showing the East Greenwich
Gas Works, which in 1965 was the world's largest gas manufacturing plant.
A Cable and Wireless ship is seen loading trans-oceanic submarine cable.

The Gypsy Moth pub and St Alfege's Church from the Cutty Sark esplanade.
The London River Commuters met every Monday in the Gypsy Moth
between 1972 and 1976.

Drawings by Neil Macfadyen illustrating Downstream to Greenwich, *by Paul Tempest.*

1989

A fortress-like folly built by Sir John Vanburgh (or Vanbrugh), the architect and dramatist, for his own occupation when he was Surveyor to the Royal Naval Hospital in 1719. Sir John lived there from 1719 to 1726. The castle is modelled on the French Bastille, where Vanbrugh was imprisoned on charges of spying for the British in 1692.

The main entrance to the Ranger's House facing onto Blackheath, viewed from the former lawns of the Greenwich Bowling Club. The back of the building faces onto the Rose Garden in Greenwich Park.

1989

Drinkers enjoying a pint outside the Union Tavern, now called the Cutty Sark. The old Harbour Master's House and Office is in the background.

A view of the *Cutty Sark* down King William Street from the north-west entrance to Greenwich Park.

If the parks be ' the lungs of London ` we wonder what Greenwich Fair is - a periodical breaking out, we suppose - a sort of spring rash.

Charles Dickens

Greenwich
Today

The Clipper, *Cutty Sark*

Launched in 1869, the *Cutty Sark* was designed to win the annual race to be the first to bring the seasonal tea harvest in China to the London market and thus secure the highest price. The voyage covered about 6,000 miles and took 90 days or more. The *Cutty Sark* never succeeded in beating the record held by the champion of the the the fleet, the *Thermopylae*, and in the year she was launched, the Suez Canal was opened, giving steamships a shortcut and immense time advantage.

The *Cutty Sark* was laid up in 1954 in her present dry dock for public display. She was gutted by fire in 2007 and reconstructed with the aim of re-opening in 2012. She sits alongside the south shaft of the Greenwich foot tunnel, completed in 1902. At high tide, the surface of the River is 53 feet (16 metres) above the lowest point of the Tunnel: when large vessels pass above, you can clearly hear the loud thump of the propellers.

"I never sailed a finer ship. At 10-12 knots she did not disturb the water at all. She was the fastest ship of her day, a grand ship, and a ship that will last for ever." Captain George Moodie, First Master of the *Cutty Sark*

Below left: a poster for the reopening of the *Cutty Sark*.

Below right: inspection of Naval cadets at the entrance to the ship.

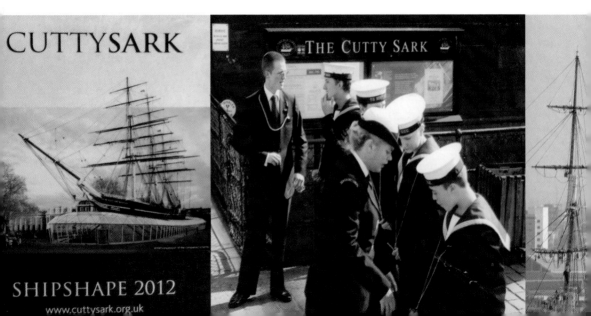

Why *Cutty Sark* was so named

Cutty Sark was one of the fastest tea-clippers of her day and well-known for sailing both in light airs and rough weather like "a witch".

The name comes from a poem by Robert Burns titled *Tam O'Shanter*. It tells the tale of a drunken farmer riding home and spotting a coven of witches beside a church on fire. Among these wrinkled hags danced a very beautiful young girl named Nannie, wearing nothing but a "cutty sark", a short linen shirt.

"Weel done, Cutty Sark!" shouted Tam.

"In an instant a' was dark," and the young girl, transformed into a mature and determined woman, turned to pursue him.

Tam knew that the only way to escape a witch was to pass over running water. He set off at full gallop. Just as he reached the nearest stream and jumped, the witch seized hold of the horse's tail and it came off in her hands. Look at the ship's figurehead (below) if you are in any doubt. This is no young girl and she has an expression of grim and murderous intent. In her outstretched hand, the horse's tail is still left there, blowing in the breeze.

Below left: the main mast of the *Cutty Sark.* being topped out in March 2012. The truck of the mast towers 152 feet above the main deck;

Below right: the *Cutty Sark* figurehead, "Nannie".

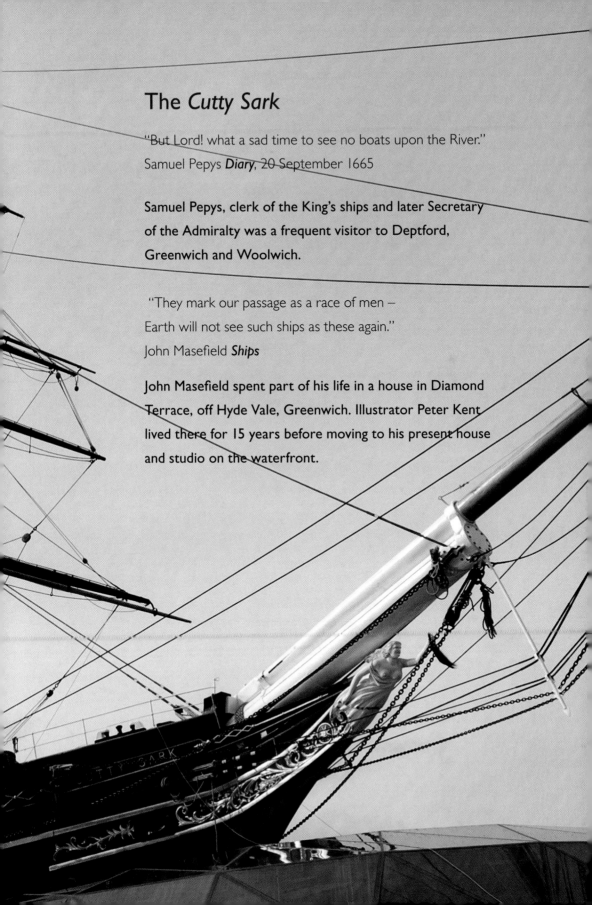

The *Cutty Sark*

"But Lord! what a sad time to see no boats upon the River."
Samuel Pepys *Diary*, 20 September 1665

Samuel Pepys, clerk of the King's ships and later Secretary
of the Admiralty was a frequent visitor to Deptford,
Greenwich and Woolwich.

"They mark our passage as a race of men –
Earth will not see such ships as these again."
John Masefield *Ships*

John Masefield spent part of his life in a house in Diamond
Terrace, off Hyde Vale, Greenwich. Illustrator Peter Kent
lived there for 15 years before moving to his present house
and studio on the waterfront.

The Royal Yacht *Britannia*

The Royal Yacht *Britannia* paying a final visit to Greenwich and London prior
to decommissioning in 1997. During her 44 years of service in the Royal Navy,
she was dedicated throughout to the service of one monarch, HM Queen
Elizabeth II.

The Royal Yacht *Britannia* passing Greenwich Pier for the last visit before lay-up in Scotland.

Trafalgar Quarters

East gate

The Chapel

The Painted

The Old Royal Naval College
and the University

Previous page: the Old Royal Naval College. The Chapel is on the left and the Painted Hall Dining Room is on the right. The master design for these magnificent buildings was drawn up by Christopher Wren and Nicholas Hawksmoor. Construction commenced in 1695 once the remains above ground of the old Royal Palace of Placentia had been cleared away. The extensive vaulted Tudor undercroft remains.

Below: the band of the Royal Marines Beating Retreat at the Old Royal Naval College. The Duke of Edinburgh took the salute as the White Ensign was lowered for the last time following a farewell Royal Navy dinner in the Painted Hall.

The Old Royal Naval College

In 1660, King Charles II commissioned the rebuilding of the dilapidated
Tudor Palace of Placentia. By 1689 when William and Mary were
crowned only one wing had been completed, the King Charles Block, and
Christopher Wren was instructed to convert and complete the site to
care for injured and retired seamen from the Royal Navy. From 1806 to
1933, the present site of the National Maritime Museum became a school
for the orphans of Royal Navy officers and men. In 1873 the Royal Navy
again converted some of the main buildings for a College for Royal Naval
Officers that eventually merged into a Joint Services Defence College and
relocated to Oxford. In 1999, after a public outcry against proposals to
accept commercial offers for the use of the site, it was handed over to the
University of Greenwich under strict conditions concerning the restoration
and maintenance of these historic buildings.

The Painted Hall

The Painted Hall, also known as the Great Hall, was constructed by Nicholas Hawksmoor between 1694-1707 to the original design of Christopher Wren. The artist James Thornhill then worked for 19 years to decorate the interior, widely considered in Europe today to be second only to the sumptuous decoration of the Vatican's Sistine Chapel. Many State Dinners and the annual Trafalgar Night Dinners are held here. Students of Trinity Laban Conservatoire of Music and Dance perform free lunch-time concerts in the Chapel on Tuesdays, and in St Alfege's Church on Thursdays.

The Painted Hall is in the King William Court, one of four blocks which formerly comprised the Royal Hospital for Seamen. It and the Queen Mary Court are both domed.

Opposite, clockwise from top left: a detail of the rear wall painting in the Lower Hall, glorifying King George I; the altarpiece by Benjamin West in the Chapel of the Queen Mary Court (refitted by James Stuart after a fire in 1779); Thornhill's magnificent painting on the west wall; a detail of one of the wall decorations in the Upper Hall; the dome (with a preliminary sketch of it shown below).

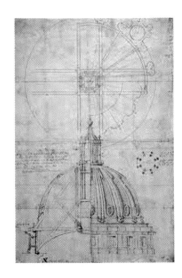

The University of Greenwich

The University of Greenwich was founded in 1992 by the amalgamation of several Polytechnics and other South East London higher education institutions, led by the Woolwich Polytechnic (founded in 1890), which had merged with the Thames Polytechnic in 1970. Building on these traditions, origins and successes, the new University has placed high emphasis on engineering, mathematics, computer technology and natural sciences. Recently it has added a very successful Business School and several other new Faculties.

With campuses spread over South East London as far as the Medway Towns, the University's administrative headquarters have, since 2000, been located in the renovated and extended Old Royal Naval College buildings on the waterfront. Co-ordination and supervision of this very rapid development has since 2004 been led by Vice Chairman Tessa Blackstone, Master of Birkbeck College.

The Trinity School of Music, now part of Trinity Laban Conservatoire of Music and Dance on the campus of the University of Greenwich, was founded in 1872. The school was located near Wigmore Street in Central London for 120 years, before moving to Greenwich in 2001.

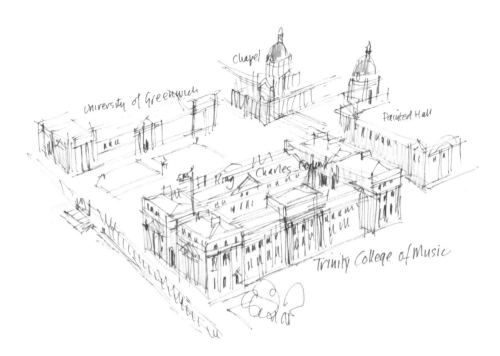

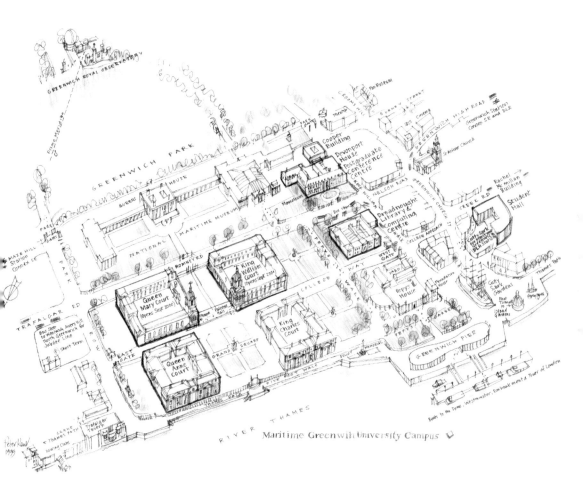

Maritime Greenwich University Campus

Lord Collingwood, Second-in-Command at the Battle of Trafalgar on 21 October 1805, is commemorated with this plaque and statue in the Royal Naval Chapel. The Chapel was completed in 1742, destroyed by fire in 1779, and promptly richly reconstructed by the classical revivalist, James Stuart, and his distinguished Clerk of Works, William Newton.

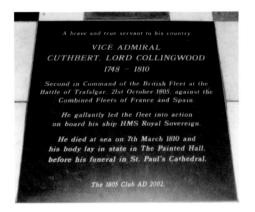

Above: the view downstream across the Grand Square extends to the O_2 Arena. On the left is the Royal Water Gate where the Sovereign is welcomed on arrival by river.

The University's new Dreadnought Library on the site of the old Dreadnought Seaman's Hospital.

The King Charles Court, begun in 1664 and now let to Trinity College of Music.

Reminders of Greenwich's naval history can be seen on the gates around the Old Royal Naval College, giving clues about the original inhabitants of the site, when it was the Royal Hospital for Seamen.

Top: the coat of arms of the Royal Hospital for Seamen is made up of four anchors with a central crown and a rope around the edge.

Middle: a gilded naval crown appears above the central gates.

Bottom: on each side gate Neptune is portrayed, with scallop shells above and below his crowned figure.

Our Visitors

Previous pages: the light aircraft carrier HMS *Invincible* (R05) was in service between 1980 and 2005, including service in the Falklands War. She was decommissioned in 2005 and scrapped in Turkey in 2011.

Above left: a visit from the Chelsea Pensioners.

Above right: visitors at the Royal Water Gate arrive at the ancient landing-point for entry into the Royal Naval College.

Bottom left: visitors at Greenwich Pier beside the southern lift-shaft of the Greenwich foot tunnel. The foot tunnel was opened in 1902 and is currently undergoing refurbishment. The Canary Wharf skyline forms an impressive backdrop.

Bottom right: in August 2011 work began on the cable car across the River to connect Greenwich Peninsula to the Royal Docks, linking two important Olympic sites. The Transport for London project, with sponsorship from Emirates and at the latest estimated costing £60 million, will be called the Emirates Air Line (Cable Car).

Ocean-going visitors moored off Greenwich

From top: MS *The World*, 644 feet, 43,524 tons, an ocean-going complex of 265 residences that circumnavigates the globe.

MS *Deutschland*, a 22,000 ton, 575-foot cruise ship that is decorated in Art Deco style.

MS *Prinsendam*, 34,848 tons, 674 feet, Holland America Line nicknamed the Elegant Explorer

MS *Seabourn Sojourn*, 32,000 tons and 650 feet, at her debut on 6 June 2010 on the River Thames. *Seabourn Sojourn* was christened by the English fashion icon and actress Twiggy.

The Borough contains eight miles of fully tidal river frontage, most of which will be accessible to the public from the Riverside Walk. The Borough also has six wharves currently reserved for cargo-handling use and two deepwater mooring sites, near the mouth of Deptford Creek and at Victoria Deep Water Terminal on the west side of Greenwich Peninsula.

Above: Trafalgar Tavern, opened in 1837, was famous for its fish suppers and Cabinet banquets, when the guests would be transported from Westminster in highly-decorated Ordnance barges to taste Greenwich whitebait and other delicacies. Distinguished diners included Charles Dickens and Samuel Pepys. To the left, Peter Kent's riverside studio can be seen.

Below: the new statue of Admiral Nelson, erected in 2009, stands looking out over the River beside the Trafalgar Tavern.

Left: some of the well-known pubs in Greenwich.

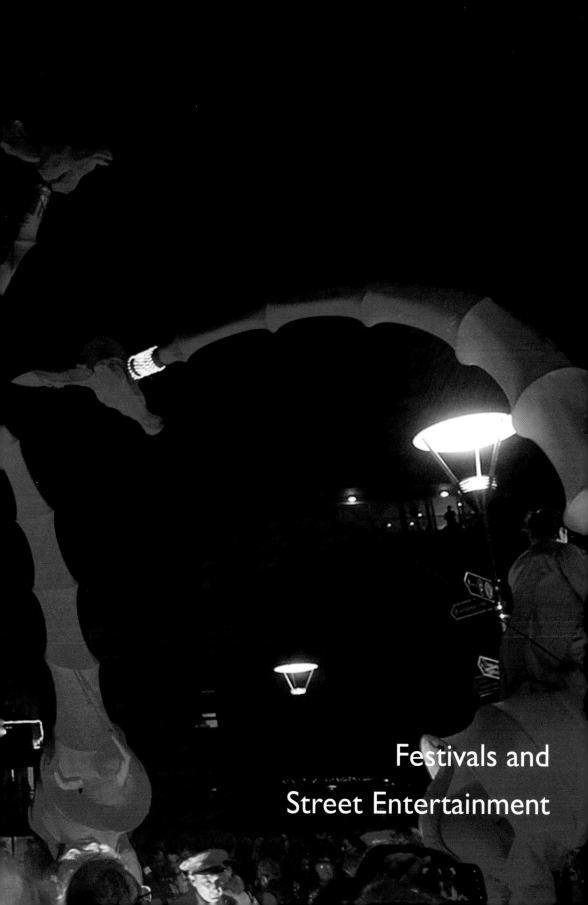

Festivals and
Street Entertainment

Greenwich Fair

Five minutes' walking brings you to the fair. The entrance is occupied on either side by the vendors of gingerbread and toys: the stalls are gaily lighted up, the most attractive goods profusely disposed, and unbonneted young ladies, in their zeal for the interest of their employers, seize you by the coat, and use all the blandishments of "Do, dear" – "There's a love" – "Don't be cross, now," etc., to induce you to purchase half a pound of the real spice nuts, of which the majority of the regular fair goers carry a pound or two as a present supply, tied up in a cotton pocket-handkerchief. Occasionally you pass a deal table, on which are exposed pen'orths of pickled salmon (fennel included), in little white saucers; oysters, with shells as large as cheese-plates, and divers specimens of a species of snail (*wilks,* we think they are called), floating in a somewhat bilious-looking green liquid. Cigars, too, are in great demand; gentlemen must smoke, of course, and here they are, two a penny, in a regular authentic cigar box, with a lighted tallow candle in the centre.

Imagine yourself in an extremely dense crowd, which swings you to and fro, and in and out, and every way but the right one; add to this the screams of women, the shouts of boys, the clanging of gongs, the firing of pistols, the ringing of bells, the bellowings of speaking-trumpets, the squeaking of penny dittoes, the noise of a dozen bands with three drums in each, all playing different tunes at the same time, the hallooing of showmen, and an occasional roar from the wildbeast shows; and you are in the very centre and heart of the fair.

This immense booth, with the large stage in front, so brightly illuminated with variegated lamps, and pots of burning fat is 'Richardson's' where you have a melodrama (with three murders and a ghost), a pantomime, a comic song, an overture, and some incidental music, all done in five and twenty minutes. The grandest and most numerously-frequented booth in the whole fair, however, is "The Crown and Anchor" – a temporary ballroom – we forget how many hundred feet long, the price of admission to which is one shilling. Immediately on your right hand as you enter, after paying your money, is a refreshment place, at which cold beef, roast and boiled, French rolls, stout, wine, tongue, ham, even fowls, if we recollect right, are displayed in tempting array. There is a raised orchestra, and the place is boarded all the way down, in patches, just wide enough for a country dance.

There is no master of the ceremonies in this artificial Eden – all is primitive, unreserved, and unstudied, The dust is blinding, the heat insupportable, the company somewhat noisy, and in the highest spirits possible: the ladies, in the height of their innocent animation, dancing in the gentlemen's hats, and the gentlemen promenading "the gay and festive scene" in the ladies' bonnets, or with the more expensive ornaments of false noses, and low crowned, tinder-box-looking hats: playing children's drums; and accompanied by ladies on the penny trumpet.

The noise of these various instruments, the orchestra, the shouting, the "scratches", and the dancing, is perfectly bewildering. The dancing, itself, beggars description – every figure lasts about an hour, and the ladies bounce up and down the middle, with a degree of spirit which is quite indescribable. As to the gentlemen, they stamp their feet against the ground every time "hands four round" begins, go down the middle and up again, with cigars in their mouths, and silk handkerchiefs in their hands, and whirl their partners round, nothing loth, scrambling and falling, and embracing, and knocking up against the other couples, until they are fairly tired out, and can move no longer. The late hour at night: and a great many clerks and prentices find themselves next morning with aching heads, empty pockets, damaged hats, and a very imperfect recollection of how it was they did *not* get home.

Charles Dickens, 1836

The Greenwich and Docklands International Festival

"An event whose annual contribution to the happiness of the people of London is unrivalled." **The Guardian**

The GDIF is an annual festival of outdoor arts, theatre, dance and family entertainment. In its 16th year in 2012, it is consistently spectacular. Events take place at sites all around Greenwich and at Canary Wharf, the Isle of Dogs, Woolwich and Mile End Park. In June of 2012 the Festival presents the world premiere of CROW (jointly commissioned by the London 2012 Festival and The Royal Borough of Greenwich), a dance theatre realisation of Ted Hughes' powerful poems by Handspring Puppet Company (of *War Horse* fame).

Until 1862, when it was closed down for being too unruly, Greenwich Fair was the largest and most uproarious outdoor gathering in London. In 2011, GDIF initiated a 21st century reinvention of the Dickensian Fair (see previous pages). A two-day outpouring of British and international street arts, Greenwich Fair proved so popular that it has become a fixture. The programme of family-friendly outdoor arts, sideshows and fun games takes place at the Old Royal Naval College, Cutty Sark Gardens, St Alfege Park, and at Greenwich Market. In April 2012, the bicentenary of Dickens' birth a month-long series of dance workshops were held by Greenwich Dance.

Pages 64-5 show Compagnie Off's astonishing "Giraffes" performance marching through the Royal Arsenal as the finale to the 2011 GIDF. Featuring a herd of life-sized, animated crimson giraffes, a team of zoo keepers, a ringmaster and an operatic diva, the production moved through Woolwich's magnificent new squares in a procession accompanied by dazzling special effects and music.

The Blackheath Donkeys

Leonard Thorne's family have been providing donkey rides at the main entrance to Greenwich Park on Blackheath for over a hundred years. His daughter Lorraine, who runs her own stables near Sevenoaks, poses, right, with the senior donkey, Humphrey, named after Duke Humphrey's Tower which stood at the other end of the Grand Avenue until 1675 when it was replaced by the Royal Observatory.

When not tending the donkeys Len writes poetry – reams of it.

BLACKHEATH DONKEYS
ODE of a DONKEYMAN

THE DONKEYS ARE HERE EVERY WEEKEND WAITING FOR THE CHILDREN TO MEET THEM ONCE AGAIN, GIVING RIDES UP AND DOWN THE PITCH AND WAITING FOR CARROTS AND TIT BITS. SO GIVE YOUR CHILD A RIDE OF A LIFETIME, A RIDE THEY NEVER FORGET, ON THAT DEAR LITTLE OLD DONKEY THEY WILL NEVER EVER FORGET. YEARS WILL GO BY WHEN THEY WILL WALK BY AND SAY: 'I RODE THAT DEAR LITTLE OLD DONKEY WHEN I WAS JUST ONLY KNEE HIGH'.

by Len the old Donkeyman

ONLY £2.00

Right: ice cream and donkeys at the main entrance to Greenwich Park on Guy Fawkes Day, 5 November 2011.

Above: at the 2011 Greenwich and Docklands International Festival the British dance theatre company Motionhouse premiered their dynamic spectacle 'Waiting Game' featuring acrobats and JCBs. Here, the dancers Vanessa Cook and Junior Cunningham perform perilously with the diggers.

Below left: Space Fiction in the park.

Below right: an exotic bird is displayed at Greenwich Pier.

Top left: the 2012 International Festival features an epic re-interpretation of the famous Greek myth *Prometheus Awakens*.

Top right: African musicians playing traditional instruments.

Middle: the St Albans Morris Men delight the crowd in Royal Place.

Bottom: the 45-foot-long polystyrene sculpture of a swimmer was commissioned for a reality television show called London Inc in 2010. Its frequent moves around London included a stay at Greenwich.

From top:

A traditional cockney Pearly King with matching London taxi cab.

Latin American musicians serenading the tourists.

A busker playing the Irish whistle.

Opposite page from top:

One of many traditional East End jazz bands who come to Greenwich to play for the London Marathon.

The Superior Brass Marching Band performing in the town centre.

A contemporary quartet sponsored by Greenwich Council play at the Park entrance.

...RINGS.CO.UK
...PES, TIPS AND ADVICE

...OW FOR OUR
...TCHERY £85
...ERCLASS
...Y JUNE 6th
...ge making
...ass.

The People of Greenwich

Previous page: Messrs Dring Family Butchers of Royal Hill.

Clockwise from top right: The Creaky Shed fruit and vegetable shop on Royal Hill displays pumpkins for Halloween.

The OREO organic café opposite the Greenwich Picturehouse on Greenwich High Road.

Spread Eagle Antiques carries on an old family calling.

Maritime Books is one of the country's foremost bookshops on naval and maritime history. Maritime Books has now moved from central Greenwich to these premises in Royal Hill.

The Cheese Board in Royal Hill attracts a regular gourmet clientèle from a wide area, and there is a specialist fresh fish shop around the corner.

Halcyon Books is a family-run secondhand bookshop in Greenwich specialising in a range of new, used and antiquarian books.

Clockwise from top right:

The Hungry Hut Café in Norman Road, where you would always get a warm smile and delicious food from Tracey, closed in November 2011, alas.

Made in Greenwich is an newly-opened, artist-run community interest company showcasing and promoting work made in, around and about Greenwich. The Hothouse @ Made in Greenwich will host workshops, storytelling, debates and videos, linking the spoken and written work with images.

The Royal Teas café on Royal Hill specialises in 'Full English' breakfasts, traditional teas with scones and home-made cakes.

The Greenwich Sea Cadets, with the London Greenwich Fire Brigade in attendance.

The weekly rubbish collection.

The milk is still delivered daily to homes and businesses in Greenwich.

MOTOR IN
858
FLORA
5025
FLORA
3669
CLAPHAM
FLORA
14270
GAZ
FLORA

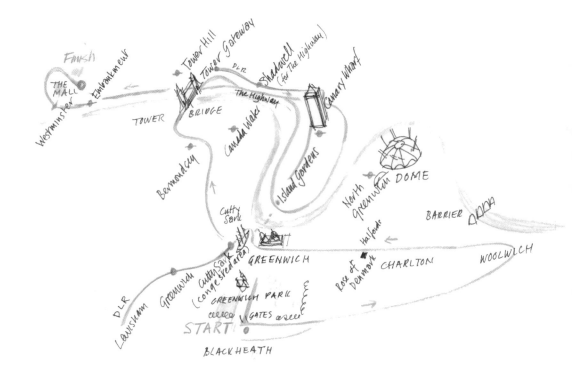

The London Marathon assembles annually in Greenwich Park on the Grand Avenue, starts eastwards on Blackheath along Shooters Hill Road, before turning left down towards the River and then left again running westwards through central Greenwich. There were 35,000 competitors in 2011 and 37,500 in 2012. The London Wheelchair Marathon (opposite, bottom) takes place on the same day – the 2012 men's and women's races were won by Britons David Weir and Shelly Woods.

Through the year there are many other such events open to the public, with shorter charity runs and walks on Blackheath and round Greenwich Park.

Central Greenwich

Previous page: the covered Central Market is open Wednesday to Sunday, and busiest at weekends and Bank Holidays.

Greenwich Railway Station was opened in 1838, when the first passenger route in Southern England provided a service from London Bridge at 15-minute intervals from 8.00 am to 9.00 pm at a cost of sixpence (omnibus or open carriage) or ninepence (1st Class, imperials or mail). By 1846, the service was carrying a million passengers per year. The station was originally located close to Greenwich Park on the assumption that the line would be continued on the surface, or by tunnel or deep cutting or on a viaduct across the Park on its planned route to Dover. When no such permission was given, the station was dismantled and rebuilt on its present Greenwich High Road site (below) in 1840.

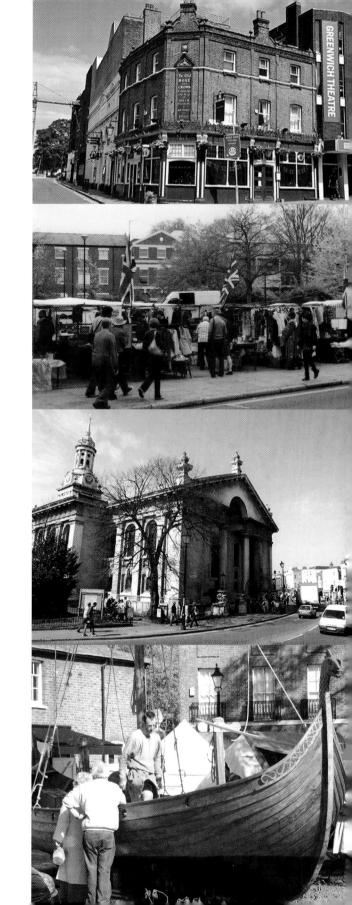

From top: Greenwich Theatre with its main entrance in Croom's Hill. The Nevada Street entrance, designed by John George Buckle, was the main entrance until 1902.

The Greenwich Clocktower Market (open weekends and Bank Holidays) has an array of quirky stalls selling antique, vintage and craft items. It is on Greenwich High Road next to the Greenwich Picture House, a five-screen cinema.

The 11th century St Alfege's Church was designed by Nicholas Hawksmoor and reconsecrated in 1718 after being destroyed by a violent storm in 1710. Alfege, Bishop of Canterbury was stoned to death here by invading Danes in 1012, exactly 1000 years ago.

On 19 April 2012, Dr Rowan Williams, the Archbishop of Canterbury, conducted a special commemorative service to mark the millennium anniversary. A re-enactment of the martyrdom of Alfege was also held, complete with replica Viking boats.

Greenwich Park

Greenwich Park

The chief place of resort in the daytime, after the public-houses, is the park, in which the principal amusement is to drag young ladies up the steep hill which leads to the Observatory, and then drag them down again, at the very top of their speed, greatly to the derangement of their curls and bonnet-caps, and much to the edification of lookers-on from below. "Kiss in the Ring" and "Threading my Grandmother's Needle", too, are sports which receive their full share of patronage.

But it grows dark: the crowd has gradually dispersed and only a few stragglers are left behind. The light in the direction of the church shows that the fair is illuminated; and the distant noise proves it to be filling fast. The spot, which half an hour ago was ringing with the shouts of boisterous mirth, is as calm and quiet as if nothing could ever disturb its serenity; the fine old trees, the majestic building at their feet, with the noble river beyond, glistening in the moonlight appear in all their beauty, and under their most favourable aspect; the voices of the boys, singing their evening hymn, are borne gently in the air.

Charles Dickens, 1836

Previous page: a 19th century view of Greenwich Park much as it is today. The Greenwich Hospital Pensioners, many of them amputees, earned extra income by acting as guides and telling naval stories. The dome of St. Paul's Cathedral is clearly visible on the horizon.

Right: spring blossom on one of the Park avenues.

THE ROYAL PARK

Whoso list to hunt, I know where is an hind . . .
And graven with diamonds in letters plain
There is written her fair neck about,
Noli me tangere, for Caesar's I am.
Sir Thomas Wyatt, c 1533

Greenwich Park is the oldest of the Royal Parks. It was enclosed in 1433, stocked with deer in 1515 and, in 1619, surrounded by a sturdy 10 foot wall, much of which remains.

King Henry VIII hunted frequently in the Park. Here he courted Anne Boleyn and planned the annulation of his marriage to Catherine of Aragon. The above verses by Sir Thomas Wyatt, another admirer of Anne, earned him the King's displeasure and he, as well as Anne, her brother and her brother's friends were

executed within a few years of Anne's coronation.

The layout of the Park follows the design of 1662 by the great French landscape architect, Andre le Notre. It has been suggested that the original plans sent to him omitted to show contours and that, as he never came to England either to look at the site or view the progress of the work, he was unaware of the hill. This may explain why the *Grand Avenue* from the Blackheath Entrance, which is accurately aligned with the Queen's

House, ends abruptly at the crest of the hill. Otherwise much of Le Notre's design remains intact. A wild part of the original Heath, *The Wilderness,* is still retained for the deer, while the hillocks and main hillside help to break up the formal pattern of the avenues and paths planted with horse-and sweet-chestnut, oak, ash and plane.

In the Spring, the enclosed area to the East of the Observatory and the Bandstand has a magnificent display of daffodils, tulips and other bulbs. The rhododendrons round the lake close by and also in the South-West corner of the Park make a fine show. Through the summer, the major floral attraction is the *Rose Garden* in front of the Ranger's House, where each of the many varieties is clearly labelled.

For the children, there are the deer in the Wilderness, wildfowl on the pond, where charts help to identify the many varieties, many squirrels and at the weekends, donkeys just outside the main Blackheath entrance. There are also ample swings and slides in the Playground and canoes and paddle-boats on the Lake both in the North-East corner. Demonstrations and talks are given regularly in the Planetarium behind Flamsteed House and free brass band concerts are given in the iron Bandstand, 18.30 in the afternoons and early evenings of Sundays in summer.

Extract from *Downstream to Greenwich – The Heritage and Future of the London* by Paul Tempest.

Right: each autumn, the Chinese gather the windfall sweet chestnuts in the Park. The oldest sweet chestnut trees were planted in the 17th century.

The Rose Garden in front of Rangers House, formerly the home of Lord Chesterfield, is beautifully tended and a riot of colour throughout the summer.

The Royal Observatory

Opposite top: a splendid cedar originating in the Lebanon beside the hillocks of the Anglo Saxon burial ground with the dome of the Royal Observatory in the background.

Opposite bottom right: one of the 17th century sweet chestnuts.

Opposite bottom left: the Royal Observatory, 1675 with the red Time Ball in the rest position atop the Octagon Room. There is a terrace café at the Royal Observatory with outstanding views of the upper park.

Below: notable trees in the park include the remains of an ancient oak, where Queen Elizabeth I played as a child, in which miscreants were held captive in the 19th century.

Time is Everything

"Time is everything – five minutes making the difference between victory and defeat."

Horatio Nelson

A Quiet Centre of Time and Space

Not until 1884 at the Treaty of Washington did the nations of the world formally acknowledge Greenwich as the base-point of the world's measurement of time and space. Even then, France refused to sign and merely added a note that everyone else had agreed to a specific point west of their own National Observatory in Paris. At Flamsteed House, where the old Royal Greenwich Observatory was established in 1675, the two most important exhibits are the telescope used to establish the line of zero longitude and the four Harrison time-pieces that first enabled Man to determine accurately his position at sea, at any time of the day or night, in any climate, location or weather.

Previous page: the Royal Greenwich Observatory, established in 1675, looking south from the Queen's House.

Left: the House of the Astronomer Royal, commissioned in 1675. The red Time Ball is raised every day, rising to the top at 12.58 and dropping at 1.00 pm precisely. One of the earliest public time signals, it was first used in 1833 and still operates today.

Below: the Victorian Planetarium building and the new Planetarium stand side by side at the Royal Observatory.

H2, pictured below, was built between 1737 and 1740 and is one of the four most important clocks in the history of navigation, all built by John Harrison (1693-1776). They were built to contend for the 1715 Longitude Prize, of £20,000, for the first person to discover a means of calculating longitude at sea. Despite meeting the full conditions, Harrison only received half the prize money from the Longditue Board in 1765 and only on condition that he surrender his clocks and plans to the Astronomer Royal, Nevil Maskelyne, who promptly consigned them to a dark damp cellar.

Top right: the 24-hour clock outside the Royal Observatory. Installed in 1852, it is one of the earliest electrically-driven public clocks. Being a 24-hour clock, the hour hand marks noon (XII) at the bottom of the dial and midnight (0) at the top.

Bottom right: the steel sculpture on the Meridian Line was installed to mark the final year of the millennium. Designed by Thinkfarm, it was sponsored by *The Times* newspaper.

Above: the The Queen's Watermen welcome *Jubilant*, a Royal Shallop, at Greenwich Pier on her maiden voyage from Kew in a 'Celebration of Time' in 2002, escorted by a flotilla of Waterman's Cutters and other historic craft. The Jubilant Trust makes use of the Shallop for training disabled rowers to join able-bodied rowers in events, ceremonies and regattas on the Thames.

Right: the 24-hour clock outside the main entrance to the Royal Observatory appears to be confusing one visitor.

Far right: tourists from all parts of the world love to be snapped standing on the Prime Meridian.

Left: the statue of James Wolfe, commander of the British forces at the capture of Quebec in 1759. After his death in the battle his body was brought back to Greenwich for burial in St Alfege's Church. The statue by Tait Mackenzie is located on the crest of the hill outside the Royal Observatory main entrance facing north. The plinth still carries the damage inflicted by a bomb during a World War Two air-raid.

The National
Maritime Museum

Previous page: the Queen's House, designed 1616 by Inigo Jones, was a gift from King James I to his wife, Queen Anne of Denmark. It straddled the London-Dover highway, running between high walls across the Royal Park. Rooms cantilevered across the highway permitted the King, Queen and Royal Courts to reach Greenwich Park from the riverside parts of the Palace without disturbing the longstanding right of way of merchants, travellers and townsfolk. The design was based on those of Palladio which Inigo Jones had seen on his travels in Italy in 1601 and 1613. Today it forms the centrepiece of the National Maritime Museum and houses an outstanding collection of marine and other paintings as well as providing a prestigious venue for major events, weddings and other celebrations.

Below: the Queen's House from Greenwich Park.

Above: the old (north) entrance of the National Maritime Museum.

Below left: the new main entrance of the National Maritime Museum, part of the Sammy Ofer Wing opened in 2011, faces Greenwich Park and has two long, constantly-running cascades of water and fine landscaping. The Museum has a popular café at the new entrance,with a gourmet restaurant on the floor above (below right).

Serene yet strong, majestic yet sedate,

Swift without violence, without terror great.

Matthew Prior

The
River
Today

Elizabeth and Leicester

Beating oars

The stern was formed

A gilded shell

Red and gold

The brisk swell

Rippled both shores

Southwest wind

Carried down stream

The peal of bells

White towers...

from *The Waste Land: Section III The Fire Sermon* (1922)

by TS Eliot (1888-1965)

Opposite: the finish of the annual Great River Race at Island Gardens opposite Greenwich. This 22-mile race used to be rowed downstream through the heart of the capital by some 250 crews in a wide variety of craft. Recently, the Race has started at Millwall to finish upriver at Ham.

Below: the North Sea Race Greenwich, 2 June 2000.

The Fairy Stream

That great common sewer of London, the Thames, a reservoir for mud, slops, slime and filth of every description, has now become a sort of fairy stream, on which our merchants, clerks, and shopmen, with their respective wives, families and mistresses, are wafted a few miles from the noise and bustle of the metropolis, in order to invigorate their smoke-dried lungs with the purer air of what they call the country. Away they go to Greenwich, Woolwich, or Gravesend, where, after dipping themselves two or three times in a creek of brackish water, they come home and preach a sermon to their friends upon the beneficial effects of sea-air and sea-bathing.

We never see a sparrow splashing about in a puddle, but we feel convinced that the creature is a cockney; it seems so happy in the littleness of its out-of-door enjoyments; and you may be perfectly certain that it was never ten miles away from London in the whole course of its life.

The crowds of happy faces on board our Thames steam-boats present us with the picture of a world in miniature; and everybody knows that the world on Sunday, unless the day be wet, is a much more joyous affair than on any other day in the week. There are married folks with their wives and families actually going to pass twelve hours together without quarrelling, simply because they are not at home, and can find abundance of novelty to amuse them. There are unmarried folks, linked arm-in-arm together, looking at the married ones and their offspring with positive envy, and thinking, poor deluded creatures, how happy they shall be when the holy banns of wedlock and the parson's blessing have allowed them to increase and multiply the number of their sympathies.

Then there is the cunning bachelor smoking his cigar in a quiet corner,
laughing in his sleeve at both, reading the Town and wondering how
people can be so silly as to take an ostensible part in the population of the
country. Here sits an old lady in a modest slate coloured silk gown, going
to Greenwich to drink tea with her younger sister; and there is a damsel in
robes of white, going to meet her lover, and spend a few delicious hours with
him in Greenwich Park. Then there's the band, playing all sorts of tunes.

The Times, Leader 1838

The River Today

So far in this book, we have given some brief impressions of how the London River had evolved from being the principal highway for people and goods through the capital since medieval times to becoming the greatest port in the world, alive with ships and shipbuilders, industry and commerce while also serving, until the late 19th century, as the city's principal sewer and source of much of its ill-health.

A low point was reached between 1940 and 1945 as the City, port and shipping became principal targets of frequent and devastating German bombing raids to be followed by a very slow post-War response in rebuilding and repairing this extensive wartime damage, of which there are still many remnants and reminders.

Over the last quarter-century, the redevelopment and rescue of the River has rapidly gained pace. The rise of the Canary Wharf high-rise buildings, among the largest in Europe, on the old Isle of Dogs and West India Docks system, has become the principal beacon for renovation, new development and new uses for the River and its immediate environment.

An important feature of this rejuvenation has been the development of the Thames Clipper services now operating between Westminster and Woolwich. These large, high-speed catamarans give a frequent and reliable service linking the 12 piers along its route both for the growing number of commuters and the very many tourists seeking a stylish and comfortable way of taking in an impression and guided tour of many of the greatest sights, buildings and monuments.

In the final part of this book, we return to the River to examine what we consider the exciting new prospects and opportunities for the London River over the next 40 years as well as the problems and risks that need to be tackled now.

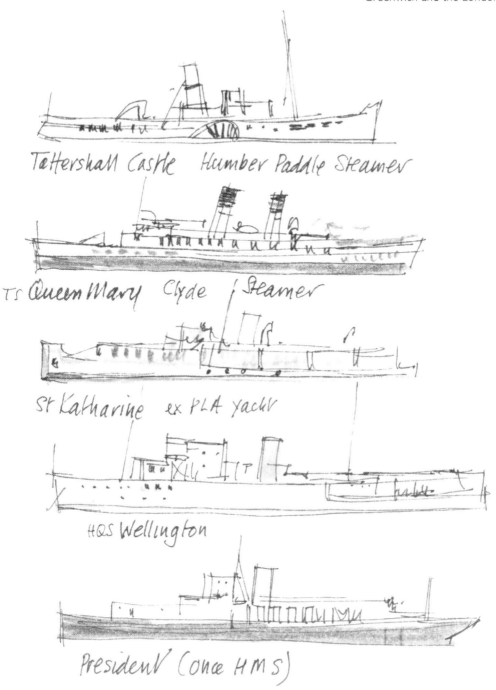

Tattershall Castle   Humber Paddle Steamer

TS Queen Mary   Clyde Steamer

St Katharine   ex PLA yacht

HQS Wellington

President (once HMS)

Historic craft moored along the Embankment. The *Wellington* has recently acquired a sliver funnel.

Now like a Maiden Queen, she will behold

From her high turrets, hourly suitors come:

The East with incense and the West with Gold ...

The silver Thames, her own domestic Floud

Shall bear her vessels like a sweeping Train.

Annus Mirabilis (1667) by John Dryden (1631-1700)

The Lord Mayor arrives at HMS President on board the Royal Shallop 'Jubilant' before the start of The Lord Mayors Show

Pages 116-7: a replica of Captain James Cook's *Endeavour* arrives under sail from Australia and New Zealand.

Top: the *Juan Sebastián de Elcano,* the Royal Spanish Navy's four-masted, steel-hulled training schooner on a visit to Greenwich.

Middle: the *Grand Turk,* a replica of a Royal Naval ship of the era of the Napoleonic wars, provides the finishing line for the annual Great River race.

Bottom: final checks on the the *Cutty Sark*'s rigging, the week before her re-opening in April 2012.

The remaining Thames sailing barges no longer carry the oats, hay and straw for London's horses from the remote creeks of Essex and Suffolk on the East Coast. Today the remaining fleet have a summer programme of racing together and many have been converted for chartering to clubs, colleges, sailing enthusiast groups and for sales promotion assignments by corporations.

Below: the new Ahoy Sailing Centre at Deptford and further development proposals.

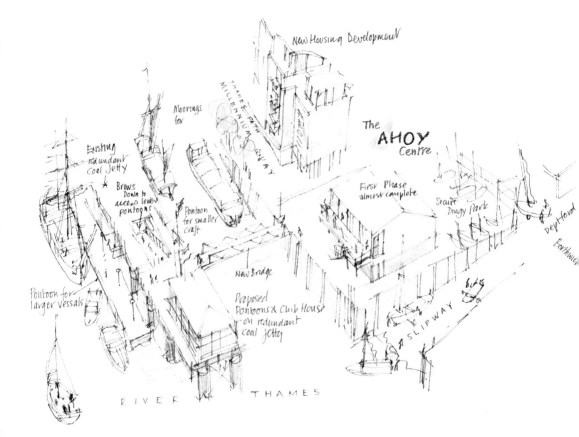

New Housing Development

Moorings for

Existing redundant coal Jetty

Brows Down to access lower pontoons

Pontoon for smaller craft

THAMES PATH MILLENNIUM WAY

The **AHOY** Centre

First Phase almost complete

Secure Dingy Park

Deptford

Earlthwick

Pontoon for larger vessals

New Bridge

Proposed Pontoons & Club House on redundant coal Jetty

SLIPWAY

R I V E R   T H A M E S

me greenwich

St Nicholas Church

Millennium Quay

Deptford Creek

Boatyard

AHOY

The Jetty

Deptford Draw dock

Peter Kent 07

The New Fast Ferries

Previous page: a KPMG Meteor Clipper in the new 2012 livery, which has superseded those seen on a Sun Clipper approaching the Millennium Bridge by Tate Modern (above), and a Hurricane Clipper by Canary Wharf (below), which bore the distinctive polka-dot livery designed by Damien Hirst.

Sir Bob Scott has been a very active Greenwich resident, much involved with the British Olympic Committee. He is Chairman of Trinity Laban Conservatoire of Music and Dance, Greenwich Theatre and South London Business.

Nick Raynsford, MP for Greenwich and Woolwich since 1997 was previously MP for Greenwich between 1992 and 1987, and for Fulham between 1986 and 1987. He was Minister for Local Government from 2001 to 2002.

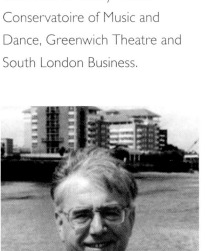

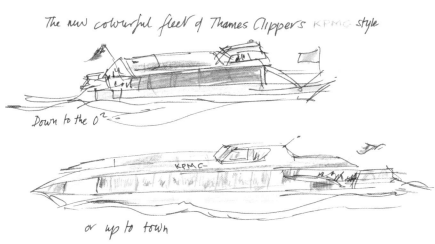

The new colourful fleet of Thames Clippers KPMG style

Down to the O²

or up to town

The High-Speed Services of 1972-77

The Italian Hydrofoils

In May 1972 the first high-speed passenger service on the London River was opened for a six-month experiment. The vessels were RHS-70, 71-seat V-foil hydrofoils constructed at the Leopoldo Rodriguez shipyard at Messina, and the service operated between Greenwich Pier and Tower Pier. There fierce battles were fought with the many private tourist boats already competing with each other for access to the piers. These new craft were not well-suited to the peculiar hazards of the tideway; trading in the livery of the Thames Arrow Express, they reached and maintained 32 knots with ease, but their splayed legs and wide foils made them quite difficult to manoeuvre alongside the boarding pontoons in conditions of strong tides, heavy swell and high winds. They were also prone to picking up large baulks of timber, small trees and discarded prams, half-submerged dinghies and the like floating in the river, resulting in these fast craft subsiding back into the water and continuing their journey at a sedate walking pace.

The British Hovercraft

The Italian hydrofoils were replaced by two, later three, British Hovermarine HM2 fixed sidewall hovercraft that had a capacity of between 60 and 65 seats and excellent reliability and manoeuverability. Their only vice was a tendency in strong wind against tide conditions to raise a skirt in a heavy swell and release a high-pressure spray of dirty Thames water over the unsuspecting tidily-suited commuters queuing patiently on the pontoon with their folded newspapers and furled umbrellas, and soaking them thoroughly. The hovercraft performed well at full capacity through the rail-strikes of 1973-74, but ceased operations as soon as the strike ended and consumer enthusiasm fell away. By then, the monthly GLC/LORICA cost-benefit analysis was beginning to give steeply negative readings.

The Russian Hydrofoils

In May 1974, two 58-seat Russian Raketa hydrofoils began a daily commuter service from Gravesend to Tower Pier and in October 1974 were switched seamlessly to replace the hovercraft on the Greenwich-Tower-Westminster service. Other Russian demonstration hydrofoils arrived, first a 102-seat Kometa and various six- to eight-seat water-taxis. The Russians also had problems with debris caught in the foils and propellers, and LORICA negotiated free vodka for all evening commuters whenever there were delays in securing a tow home.

The US Jetfoil

Finally, from June 1977, a 42-knot 110-ton Boeing Jetfoil with a seating capacity of 200 passengers was was tried out on the river and given a license to run a daily service from St Katherine's Pier to Zeebrugge, taking three-and-a-half hours each way. There were navigational concerns about such large vessels travelling fast in narrow channels and over old tunnels, and the service was suspended.

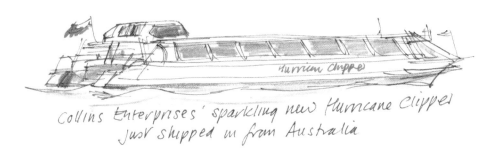

Collins Enterprises' sparkling new Hurricane Clipper
just shipped in from Australia

Above: the Thames Arrow (1972-1973) was a revolutionary Italian design, but the projecting hydrofoil caused problems at the piers.

Below: the Russian Kometa (1973-1974) replaced the Thames Arrow. It proved to be too unwieldy and was replaced by two smaller Russian Raketas.

Above: from July 1973 to October 1974, three British sidewall hovercraft provided daily services between Westminster, Tower Pier and Greenwich. In the background is the Danish Royal Yacht on a visit to the Royal Naval College.

Below: in June 1977, a new high-speed daily services down the Thames was inaugurated between St Katharine's Pier and Zeebrugge, taking three-and-a-half hours each way using a US 42 knot, 110-ton Boeing Jetfoil, the Flying Princess, with a capacity of 200 passengers.

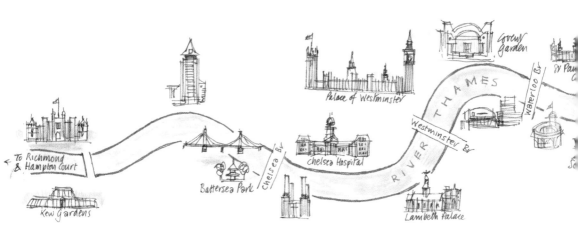

The London River from Hampton Court to the Thames Barrier.

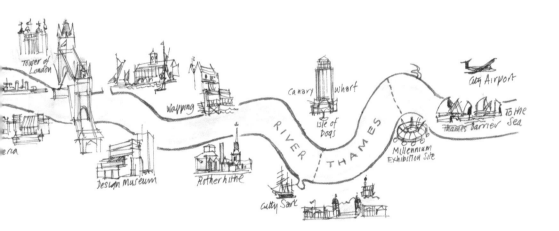

Tower of London

Wapping

Canary Wharf

Isle of Dogs

RIVER THAMES

City Airport

Thames Barrier

To the Sea

Millennium Exhibition Site

Design Museum

Rotherhithe

Cutty Sark

Down the River:
Snapshots from
Westminster to Greenwich

Above: Westminster Bridge with the Houses of Parliament beyond. To the right are the twin towers of Westminster Abbey and Portcullis House, the new administration building with conference and meeting facilities for members of the Houses of Parliament and senior officials.

Below: Festival Pier and the Royal Festival Hall, the heart of the Southbank Centre.

Above: the London Eye at Waterloo on the South Bank.

Below: HMS *President*, lies alongside the Embankment close to Blackfriars Bridge and Pier. Formerly HMS *Saxifrage*, she is an Anchusa class sloop, completed in 1918. Her funnel was repainted silver in 2011. To the right, the Gherkin tower is in the heart of the City of London.

Above: St Paul's Cathedral from the London Millennium Footbridge. The bridge links the North Bank near the Cathedral with the South Bank adjacent to the Tate Modern art gallery, which is housed in the shell of the old Bankside Power Station.

Below: the central White Tower of the Tower of London, completed by King William (the Conqueror) in 1086.

Above: the Shard Tower beside London Bridge in April 2012, as it nears completion.

Below: HMS *Belfast*, when launched the largest cruiser built for the Royal Navy, entered service in 1939. She was severely damaged by a German mine in the Firth of Forth in 1940. She took part in the destruction of the German warship *Scharnhorst* in1944 and in the Korean War in 1950-2.

A view from the Isle of Dogs.
A view of East Greenwich riverfront
from Island Gardens (formerly
Scrapiron Park). This commercial area
is now gradually being redeveloped.

Top: entrance to St Katharine's Dock, built in 1828. The dock is still in use as a yacht marina, attracting many visitors on account of its proximity to Tower Bridge and the Tower of London.

Top middle: HMS *President*, small-boat headquarters of the Royal Navy in London, just beyond St Katharine's Dock on the north shore.

Bottom middle: headquarters of the London River Police at Wapping. The vessels are serviced in a new hangar projecting over the water just to the left of this photograph

Bottom: the 'Royal Nore' one of the Port of London launches used to patrol the River from Teddington lock to the sea and to transport the Queen and visiting VIPs up and down the River.

Cuckold's Point

A Frolick to Horn Fair, Greenwich October 1700

"At Cuckold's Point, we went into the House, where the Troop of Merry Cuckolds us'd to Rendesvous: Arm'd with Shovel, Spade or Pick-Ax; their Heads adorn'd with Horned Helmets; and from thence to March, in Order, for Horn-Fair ..."

This account of the origin of the name of Cuckold's Point and of the great medieval annual fairs on Blackheath tells the story of how King John of England (1199-1216), passing this way, fell in love with the Miller's wife and resolved to take her to bed.

"...when an Opportunity stood fair, the Dame consented; but as 'tis believ'd, so cunningly arrang'd the matter, that her Husband should come Home and Catch 'em in the height of their Passion; which the Miller did accordingly; and seeming not to know that he was King, took him up in his Arms and Theaten'd to fling him into the Mill-Dam, and Grind his Head off..."

His Majesty was said to be so frightened that, in exchange for his life and freedom, the Miller would be given all the land he could see from his mill looking downriver on the south side provided the King was immediately released unharmed. The only condition was that the Miller:

"...should once a Year, upon that day Twelve-month, which prov'd the 18th of October, Walk to the farthest bound of his Estate with a pair of Bucks-horns on his Head, attended with all his Family, or in Neglect of which, the Land should be forfeited..."

The Miller washed his eyes carefully and looked downwards and saw as far as Charlton-Hill embracing all of Rotherhithe, Deptford, Greenwich and Blackheath:

"...all which Land he afterwards Enjoy'd, only performing the aforementioned Ceremony, according to Agreement: and it is said that there are Lands hereabout that are held even to this Day after the same manner".

Printed and Sold by J How, the Ram-head Inn Yard, in Fenchurch Street, London

Top left: William Pye's sculpture titled *Curlicue* represents the Thames and is sited prominently at the entrance to the Greenland Dock, Rotherhithe.

Top right: the Harbour Master's House on Ballast Quay, East Greenwich.

Bottom: new flats on the Isle of Dogs opposite the Cutty Sark pub, not dissimilar to medieval fortifications.

I am the ghost of Shadwell Stair

Along the wharves by the water-house,

And through the dripping slaughter-house,

I am the shadow that walks there.

Yet I have flesh both firm and cool,

And eyes as tumultuous as the gems

Of moons and lamps in the lapping Thames

When dusk sails wavering down the pool.

Shuddering the purple street arc burns

Where I watch always, from the banks

Dolorously the shipping clanks

And after me a strange tide turns.

From *Shadwell Stair,* 1912 by Wilfred Owen (1898-1984)

Right: the Shadwell Sailing Club's safety boat with a sailing dinghy beyond.

Shadwell on the North Bank

Shadwell, on the North Bank where the River turns sharply to the right opposite Cuckold's Point, was notorious through the 19th century for stripping the incoming sailors of their pay after discharge from their ships – whether by the entertainments of bear-baiting, cock-fights and the like or by assault after heavy drinking, feasting, gambling and carousing in the many taverns and public houses.

The rude and savage enjoyments of Shadwell

A tug spurts smoke in your face. They are dancing on the deck of the Gravesend boat. The stern-faced Thames police are pulling vigorously from under our bows. There is hoarse and coarse comment from the bridge of our good ship, delivered by the river pilot, and addressed to a pleasure party in a wherry, making for the rude and savage enjoyments of Shadwell.

From *London – A Pilgrimage*, 1872 by Gustave Doré and Blanchard Jerrold

Greenwich to Woolwich

Previous page: a vivid illustration of Greenwich's maritime diversity – the *Portwey*, a traditional Thames tug passes the Damien Hirst-liveried Clipper. Between the Blackwall Rowing Club and the Clipper, a Thames barge is moored.

Rowing at Greenwich

Under the patronage of the three rival rowing clubs at Greenwich, Poplar RC on the North Bank and the Curlew RC and Globe RC at Greenwich on the South Bank, there is much interest in rowing on the tideway in single and double sculls, and in fours and eights. The highlight of the annual rowing calendar falls in September each year when the Great River Race brings several hundred oarsmen and women to row through Central London.

Below: Greenwich from Island Gardens across the River, a view unchanged for over 250 years.

Celebrations at Greenwich and Deptford

Among the many sea-borne visitors, there is a centuries-old tradition, a special welcome for distinguished sailors and historic vessels. Here at Deptford Queen Elizabeth I knighted Francis Drake in 1581 following his circumnavigation of the globe in 1577-80 and in June 1967 Queen Elizabeth II knighted Francis Chichester at Greenwich following his solo circumnavigation in *Gipsy Moth IV* – using the same sword that Queen Elizabeth I had used in 1581.

Below: the *Grand Turk*, a Napoleonic Wars replica man-of-war was built in Turkey for a 'Hornblower' adventure film. On a visit from her mooring in France she is seen midstream in the Thames at Greenwich.

The Thames Barrier

Reflections on the Thames Barrier: A Conundrum

The Thames Barrier at Woolwich was completed in 1983, 30 years after the Great Flood of 1953 caused the loss of 300 lives, the displacement of 100,000 residents from 24,000 inundated houses and flats, and immense agricultural damage on the East Coast and in the Thames Estuary. Some 200 miles of railway, 12 gasworks and two large power-stations were put out of action.

Central London had escaped by a whisker with only minor flooding and water levels in the River just inches below the parapet walls on either bank. Calculations of the scale of damage if the flood level had been only a foot or two higher concluded that over one million residents would have been flooded out with disastrous consequences for the stability of buildings, extensive damage to the underground railway system, disruption of the capital's roads and surface transport network and a heavily reduced supply of electricity, fresh water and gas. The excellent Victorian sewage system would have been overwhelmed with back-flooding of effluent into many houses and a huge noxious spillage into the tideway. There would also have been major damage to London's river-based manufacturing industry and port facilities, only just beginning to recover from the heavy bombing by the Luftwaffe in World War Two. As most of the emergency generators and essential communications equipment were located below ground in the new high-rise developments and most older buildings in the Westminster area, the Government itself would have lacked the ability to coordinate an adequate response to such a disaster when many of its own departments and buildings were flooded and out of action.

Tackling a Heightened Risk

A general consensus quickly emerged that protection of the capital was an urgent priority, but there was deep disagreement on how that protection could be provided.

The Dutch, who for centuries had led the world in the science of building dams, dredging and river management, pointed to their successes in recovering large estuary areas for agriculture, new industry and residential development by the construction of huge sea-defences, some more than 20 miles long. The technical solution they advocated was a permanent barrier or barrage with shipping locks and dredged access to be located in the vicinity of Southend on the north side of the Thames Estuary and Sheerness on the south side. Alternatively, a similar barrier might be constructed where the River was much narrower close to Tilbury on the North Bank and Gravesend on the south side, but the problem here was the narrowness of the shipping channel and the curvature of the River which affected the siting of the new locks.

Previous page: the Thames Barrier from downstream on the south side of the River.

Opposite: the Control Tower of the Thames Barrier.

Below: an accident at the Barrier in October 1997 when the *Sand-Kite*, an aggregate dredger, misjudged its approach and became firmly jammed in one of the gates.

Imports and Exports Prevail

Apart from the necessary commitment of vast Government resources to achieve such an objective, there were other difficulties of a political, economic and commercial nature facing the British Government in 1953. The Port of London dock system, despite the extensive damage sustained during 1940 to 1945, was still the largest such system in the world. Through it passed the largest share of total imports of food and manufactures into the United Kingdom. To these totals had to be added the essential imports of oil for the Thames refineries downstream, a large amount of coal for the London coal-fired power-stations and materials for a wide variety of industry and construction sector activity along the Thames. Heavy emphasis was being placed at this time on the need to pay for steeply rising imports through new export capacity, much of it located on or near the Thames. At that time also, regular passenger ferry services to Europe and long-distance routes all over the world brought large streams of passengers in both directions. Any interruption in this passenger and freight traffic and impeded access on the River caused by barrage or barrier construction would have had dire effects on post-war economic recovery. There were also coldwar security issues: vast locks and vulnerable earth barriers would, in the event of war, present an indefensible target for long-range ballistic missiles, whether conventional or nuclear.

The Next Best Solutions

By 1972, when I first became involved in these matters, the die had just been cast by the Thames Barrier and Flood Prevention Act that received Royal Assent in August 1972. The decision had been taken to construct a multi-gate barrier at Woolwich on the basis of the following logic:

• London was indeed highly vulnerable to surge-tide flooding and a reliable system of protection was necessary and urgent.

• There could be no impediment to the free flow of shipping up and down the Thames.

• The construction of a downriver earth dam would be too costly and take too long to build. Studies of the consequences in terms of silting and the need for continuous dredging of the shipping channels above and below the dam ruled out this option.

• The construction of a multi-gate barrier from Tilbury to Gravesend would greatly inhibit the development of the new post-war dock facility at Tilbury which was already bedevilled by the awkwardness of its tidal entry that imposed limits on the size and number of vessels capable of entering the dock on each high tide. This difficult manoeuvring also interfered with the free passage of large vessels to and from the upriver docks

• The multi-gate barrier at Woolwich was the next-best solution. The ideal site would involve the closure of the Tate & Lyle sugar refinery, the largest in Western Europe and its deep-water unloading berths in the River. Once the Government had realised the scale of compensation to be claimed by the company, they settled on the present site. An important factor here was that the necessary building land on either side of the barrier was readily and cheaply available.

Left: the Thames Barrier open for maritime traffic.

Thames: Sacred River

"In the reaches before Lechlade the water makes its way through isolated pastures; at Wapping and Rotherhithe the dwellings seem to drop into it, as if overwhelmed by numbers. The elements of rusticity and urbanity are nourished equally by the Thames. That is why parts of the river induce calm and forgetfulness, and others provoke anxiety and despair. It is the river of dreams, but it is also the river of suicide. It has been called liquid history because within itself it dissolves and carries all epochs and generations. They ebb and flow like water."

Peter Ackroyd, from *Thames: Sacred River* (Chatto & Windus, London 2007, pp.490)

Peter Ackroyd has published 26 books including *London: The Biography, The Great Fire of London, Dan Leno and the Limehouse Golem* and biographies of Chaucer, Shakespeare, Thomas More, Newton, JMW Turner, Dickens, Blake, TS Eliot and Ezra Pound, all of which feature the London River and the people of the River Thames.

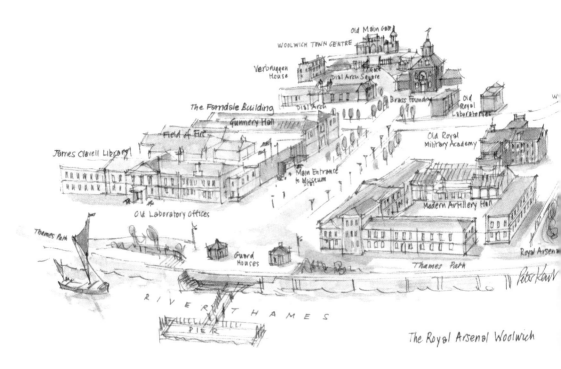

The Royal Arsenal Woolwich

The Woolwich Free Ferry

The Woolwich Ferry was established in the 14th century following the granting of a Royal privilege. In 1889 large vessels were provided to carry vehicles, passengers and goods. A fleet of paddle steamers was finally retired in the 1960s and replaced by the present generation of double-ended roll-on roll-off vessels. The ferry service provides an essential link between the Eastern ends of the North and South Circular roads which in the West are linked across the River by Kew Bridge.

Right: a photograph from the 1960s showing the old and new ferries.

Bottom left: the *Ernest Bevin*, built in Dundee in 1963. She is one of the three diesel ferry boats that replaced the old paddle steamers She and her identical sister boats *John Burns* and *James Newman* entered service in 1963 and remain in use to this day.

Bottom right: the Tate & Lyle sugar refinery facilities at Silvertown on the North Bank.

Do not despair
For Johnny – head-in-air;
He sleeps as sound
As Johnny underground.

Fetch out no shroud
For Johnny – in-the-cloud;
And keep your tears
For him in after years.

Better by far
For Johnny-the-bright-star,
To keep your head,
And see his children fed.

For Johnny by John Pudney (1909-1977)

John Pudney, an RAF intelligence office, lived in McCartney House, home of General James Wolfe, at the upper western entrance to Greenwich Park. Pudney was a distinguished authority on the history of the London River and the London Docks. This, his most famous poem, was written on the back of an envelope during an air raid in 1941 for the many Battle of Britain pilots who failed to return from combat.

Sir Winston Churchill (1874-1965)

"We shall not flag or fail. We shall go on to the end. We shall fight in France, we shall fight on the seas and oceans, we shall fight with growing confidence and growing strength in the air, we shall defend our island, whatever the cost may be. We shall fight on the beaches, we shall fight on the landing grounds, we shall fight in the fields and the streets, we shall fight in the hills; we shall never surrender." **(Speech in the House of Commons, 4 June 1940)**

"Never in the field of human conflict was so much owed by so many to so few." **(Tribute to the skill and courage of British airmen in the recent battle as delivered in the House of Commons, 20 August 1940)**

Woolwich is the traditional home of the Royal Artillery and former premier munitions centre in the Royal Dockyard. Displays in the Royal Artillery Museum, now located within the Royal Dockyard, are enlivened by RA ceremonies, presentations, demonstrations and celebrations of key events.

Family Sailing on the London River

Greenwich our Home

In 1963 the Tempest family settled in Greenwich close to the River and the Park and, apart from three assignments abroad, we – myself, my wife Jennifer, and our children Stephen, Clare and Susie – have stayed in the area ever since.

Betwen 1972 and 1976 we helped set up the London River Commuter Association to support the new commuter services between Greenwich, Tower Pier and Westminster and this led to a continuing dialogue with the Port of London Authority, the Greater London Council and various Government departments.

In 1992-2004 we kept our boat in commission each winter in the South Dock at Rotherhithe, day-sailing through each winter between Tower Bridge and the Barrier and in summer taking a mooring on the Medway opposite Upnor Castle or on the Crouch at Burnham. Family summer holidays began and ended with calls at Ramsgate and Boulogne before cruising down the Normandy coast or to the Solent.

This book is dedicated to our three grandchildren

Amy (born 2000)   Jo (born 2003)   Jake (born 2012)

Previous page: *Becky*, the family sail-boat, entering the South Dock, Rotherhithe, after her annual cruise to the East Coast, Solent and Normandy.

Page 161: a view from *Becky* of Canary Wharf in 2001.

September 2001

One thing stood out between my friends and me at school – summer holidays. While my friends jetted off to exotic shores in Greece and what was then known as Yugoslavia, I was often to be found barricaded in harbour at Portsmouth waiting for the tail end of a hurricane to pass, I wondered what I had done to deserve such hardship.

Every year, as I returned to school in September, my friends would be glowing with Mediterranean tans and stories of Greek waiters who had promised them the world. And all I could offer were stories of rats in Cherbourg marina and, if I was lucky, the odd glance from an Adonis at Cowes Week.

Now the tables have turned. As I sit loosely chained to my desk in the City, Mum, Dad and Stephen tease me with their latest experiences of supper at Chez Jules in Boulogne or dodging between the giant ships in the Solent during the Admiral's Cup. And all I can think of is escaping at the weekends on *Becky* and how to get the best sailing out of what feels like a very short summer.

It was Tuesday, 11 September 2001 and Dad had managed to fit in the last proper sail of the summer – from Chatham Dockyard and home to Rotherhithe. I was at work and had been jealous, knowing that I would have to wait until Spring 2002 to sail the English Channel again. The news of the terrorist attacks in the US broke in the early afternoon. Work became irrelevant and my colleagues and I scrabbled for every scrap of information and tried to make sense of these inhuman acts. I tried desperately to get hold of Dad and even when I finally relayed the terrible news, I could not express the enormity of what had just happened. Now, only two weeks after the attacks, I feel comfort that for a few hours my father, sailing up Old Father Thames, was blissfully unaware of the events that had changed the world. Let us hope that London remains free of such a calamity.

Susie, Tuesday, 21 September 2001

I must go down to the seas again, to the lonely sea and the sky,

And all I ask is a tall ship and a star to steer her by,

And the wheel's kick and the wind's song and the white sail's shaking,

And a grey mist on the sea's face, and a grey dawn breaking.

I must go down to the seas again, for the call of the running tide

Is a wild call and a clear call that may not be denied.

And all I ask is a windy day with the white clouds flying,

And the flung spray and the blown spume, and the sea-gulls crying.

I must go down to the seas again, to the vagrant gypsy life,

To the gull's way and the whale's way where the wind's like a whetted knife;

And all I ask is a merry yarn from a laughing fellow-rover,

And quiet sleep and a sweet dream when the long trick's over.

Sea Fever by John Masefield, (1878-1967) 1902

Clockwise from top: *Becky Seacracker* snug in Ramsgate Harbour.

Jo, our granddaughter, at the helm of *Becky Seacracker* (safely tied up in Ramsgate).

The Dome (now the O$_2$ Arena) with new buildings under construction at Canary Wharf.

The Erith Yacht Club, a useful stopover on passages up and down the River.

Stephen at the helm, en route to Queenborough at the mouth of the Medway.

Our own exotic mermaid, Elda Brizuela of Costa Rica, intent on luring the River Police Patrol for a closer inspection.

Jennifer aboard *Becky* as they pass Greenwich Pier and the Royal Naval College.

Ondine of Arne, our previous boat, designed by Olin Stephens of New York, at Burnham-on-Crouch.

Channel Stew

We had very many happy times sailing together, but it wasn't all rose-coloured. There were strong river smells, hot water limited to a few drops from the kettle, damp towels and crumpled spare clothes, Dad's awful channel stews, soggy cornflakes, sour fresh milk or old long-life, rats on the foreshore, the bow-hump (protest sessions with my sister in the bow), hard aground at Brightlingsea, deck leaks, smelly diesel engines, no TV, no fridge, no telephone, no heating, late-night arrivals after the shops had shut, early morning departures before they opened, sodden sails dumped in the cabin, sinister flotsam, fog, snow, freezing ritual trips down to the Barrier on Boxing Day and over the New Year, disputed landfalls, confusing lights, detergent bubbles and worse in Boulogne, and the wind howling and rain sheeting down in some god-forsaken muddy Essex creek.

Susie, March 2012

Right: cartoons drawn by Clare Tempest depicting family life on their numerous boat outings and cruises.

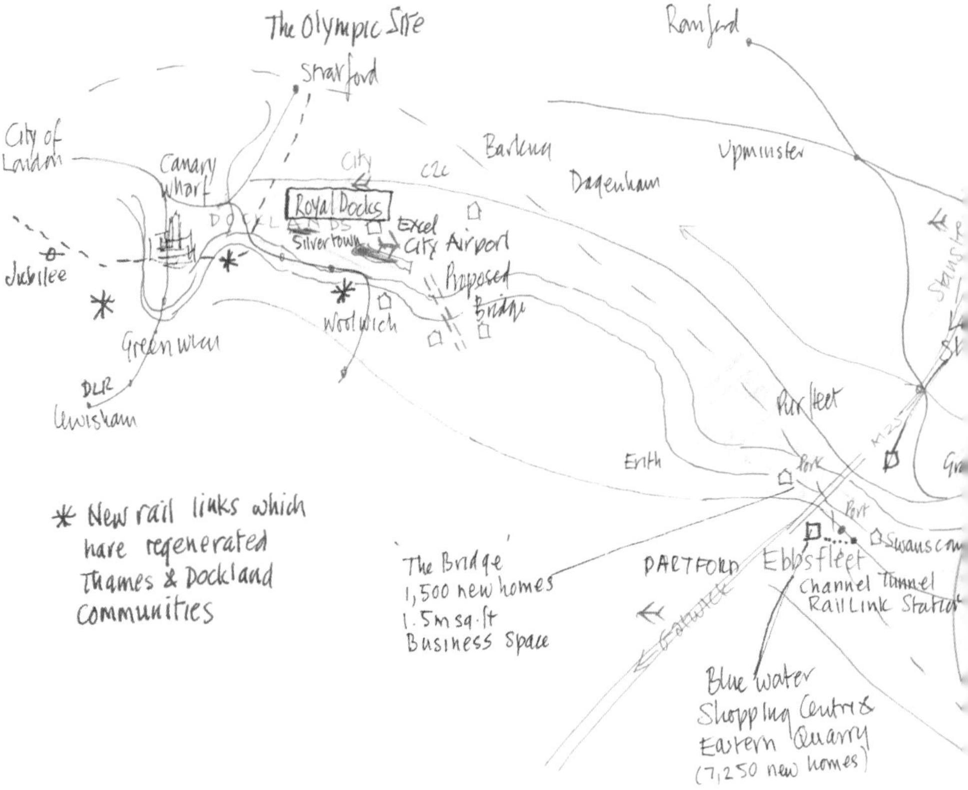

major new waterside city
tractive to international business
a similar size as the square mile
d Canary Wharf, attracting
illed workforce of the region
m both sides of the river with
new rail link serving cross river
mmunities old and new

THAMES GATEWAY
Cross River Regeneration

c2c
Basildon

aindon

Rayleigh
Benfleet

SOUTHEND

Southend

RIVER ROACH

A13

d's Water City
Ilbury
c2c
Passenger Freight

Proposed London Gateway
Container Port

coryton

Canvey

SOUTHEND
c2c

Shoebury Ness

Pier

Major
wind farms
London
Array off
Clacton
margate

Foster's Airport

Possible
North/South
Rail Link

reseud

Major waterside
developments

Isle of Grain

Farrells Gateway

Medway
Tunnel

Freight

Port

Thames Port

Port
Sheerness

SHEPPEY

Rochester

Chatham MEDWAY

MEDWAY
TOWNS

Gillingham

m2

New
Bridge

SWALE

Sittingbourne

M2

The Future of the London River

What Could Happen to Old Father Thames?
Forty years back and forty years forward

Introduction

In 1972, the London River Commuters Association (LORICA) was founded in Greenwich to assist the new high-speed passenger services then being established between Greenwich and Central London. These trials provided a continuous commuter service on the River for four years by three separate operators in turn, but failed to develop into a frequent, cheap, reliable and fast service serving the various commuting communities up and down the River. Attempts have been made since to revive the water buses which provided a popular but slow service during the Festival of Britain in 1951. Only within the last ten years has the new fleet of high-speed Australian-built catamarans been able to expand the services to many new piers and to provide frequent and reliable services from early-morning to late-evening.

Meanwhile, LORICA became involved with other consumer issues on the River - repeated heavy overflows of raw sewage, dumping of rubbish, lack of passenger piers, leisure access, Port of London spending estimates and Greater London long-term policy issues. On 8 August 1975 I set out the views of LORICA in The Times under the above heading and on the same day launched Downstream to Greenwich, The Heritage and Future of the London River.

The London River Today

Forty years on, the London River is springing back to life with much new development, a improved rail, underground, road and river transport infrastructure and a much more sympathetic and positive public opinion. This is already a story of piecemeal success, a lot of it unsung, but today there are new pressing problems and some long-term issues have yet to be resolved. In the year of the London Olympics, where Greenwich, Woolwich and the London River play an important part, we are publishing here and in detail elsewhere, our thoughts on the options for the next forty years ahead. Clothed in the guise of another of our family guides to Greenwich and the London

River, we hope this book will highlight some of the deeper, longer-term truths about the River that are in danger of being over-looked.

Our Conclusions Between 1972 and 1975

In our 1972-75 meetings, publications and reports, we focussed on various Dutch engineering studies on the need for full control of rivers from either end and on how public confidence could be restored by full ample flood prevention and protection that was clearly lacking on the upper and tidal Thames at that time. Starting upstream, the provision of new reservoirs and designated flood plains would greatly restore general confidence and also enhance London's water-supply. Downstream, with the Thames Barrier Act, prompted by the disastrous East Coast floods of 1953, only reaching the Statute Book in 1972, detailed design and construction still lay ahead. Also there had been only limited and delayed response in repairing the damage of repeated heavy bombing of the docks in World War Two and much despair, delay and neglect in the immediate post-war period. The London dockers saw their livelihood disappearing to new facilities downstream to Tilbury (privatised in 2002) and to the highly efficient new ports of Rotterdam and Felixstowe and the widespread mechanisation of cargo-handling through the use of containers. As for the general public, they were largely ignorant of the high pollution in the River and the extent of the deterioration of the shore-line on either side.

Our thoughts triggered an outcry from some river-side residents in Middlesex, Surrey, Berkshire, Buckinghamshire and Oxfordshire accompanied by some expressions of support from Greenwich, Essex and the East End. This, however, was as nothing to the negative but sentimental response country-wide to a suggestion that if the flow of the River could be fully controlled and channelled and London fully protected from the effects of excessive rainfall and freak tidal surges, there would be room for an eight or even ten-lane motorway straight up the river-bed from Dartford to Kew. We were not surprised, concluding that such a response was probably based on deeply-held sentiment and affection for the River Thames. Instead what we all got was continuing floods from time to time upriver and, formally opened in 1984, a very expensive Thames Barrier, a beautiful piece of design and engineering that has provided effective temporary protection but that was built in the wrong place to the wrong out-dated specifications.

The Thames Barrier

The snag with the classic repeated Dutch advice to construct an earth barrage well downstream with locks was that, in 1953, the year of the disastrous East Coast floods and heavy loss of life in the Netherlands, the Port of London was still the largest in the world and the fragile UK economy was dependent on the Port of London for a high proportion of its imports and exports and for its valuable entrepot trade. It was considered essential to keep this tidal river fully open to shipping day-in, day-out. This conundrum, confusion and conflict was put by the Government to their designated Chief Scientific Adviser, Professor Sir Hermann Bondi, who quickly declared that the exposure of London to massive damage by a tsunami-like tidal surge was a very real risk and full protection was an urgent priority. He ruled out earthen dams in the outer estuary given that the very large gates and dams necessary would be at the edge of technology and very difficult to assemble and operate in open water. Add to this, very high cost, a long construction period, vulnerability during construction and operation and accompanying delays to shipping. Time was of the essence in minimising risk.

He then looked at four sites within the River, one at Gravesend, two at Dagenham and one at Crayfordness, roughly half-way between Woolwich and Gravesend. Again he concluded that the large drop-gates or swing-gates or retractable barriers proposed were all too clumsy and risky while shipping movements, given the sharp curves in the course of the River, would be severely restricted.

Moving upstream he favoured three sites in the Woolwich reach. The centre site seemed ideal, but would involve dismantling the Tate & Lyle Sugar Refinery, the largest in Western Europe and rebuilding it elsewhere. The Eastern site was considered too close to the Woolwich Free vehicle and passenger ferry and a sharp curve in the River that would present an additional hazard for ships lining themselves up to pass through one of the gates of the Barrier. When the Tate & Lyle claim for compensation was received, it was decided to go for the present Western site, where the land could be purchased quite easily and cheaply. The winning design provided for four main navigation openings, two of them 200-feet wide and the other two 100-feet wide, all with rising sector gates. To allow the free flow of the tide, there are four more openings of 100 feet fitted with falling radial gates. Thus, in principle, four large vessels and two small ones could pass through the Barrier simultaneously at any time when the Barrier was open. When it was fully closed, the Barrier would present a continuous curved face to the incoming tide from one side of the River to the other.

By the time the Barrier was formally opened in 1984 (and by then the flood defences on both sides of the Thames and up the East Coast had been raised at great expense and effort), there was no longer any need for six separate shipping channels and gates. The Surrey Dock system had closed and there were very few vessels still using the other docks upriver of the Barrier and many of their port loading, unloading and warehousing facilities were entering the phase of terminal decay, abandonment, demolition or conversion to other uses.

The Risk of Surge-Tide Flooding Remains

Between 1974 and 1980, it was calculated that one million people living in 350,000 dwellings in an area of 75 square miles and the one-and-a-half million working population in this stricken area were at risk. Flooding to a considerable depth would take place in a period of less than an hour. All basements within the danger area would be flooded, with widespread cessation of electricity supply and contamination from released sewage. The water-level would be ten feet (more than three metres) above ground-level in the worst affected areas. There would be massive damage to property, infrastructure, power stations and industry and the entire central sector of the underground between Hammersmith, Stratford, King's Cross and Clapham would be flooded and out of action for up to a year. In the 1953 flood there were 307 deaths in the UK, with a heavy toll on Canvey Island on the North

Bank. Given the high level of development on both sides over the last 30 years, it would be prudent to think of material damage in real terms at a high multiple of the earlier estimates and a much higher number of fatalities, if, for some reason, the Barrier failed to close and the freak tidal surge was much above previous levels.

A Delicate Matter

Since 1980, the first new high-rise buildings such as at Canary Wharf have settled more into the London clay than was planned, while high spring-tide levels are well above and are much more frequent than what had been expected in 1972-84. The complex machinery of the Thames Barrier will not last for another forty years without significant and costly upgrading and very careful maintenance while the terrorist risk can only be met by diligent and prompt security, and rigorous police and military contingency arrangements. Understandably, the authorities are reluctant to alarm the public unduly, and rightly continue to regard their emergency response procedures as highly confidential.

Accidents can also happen. One vessel approaching the Barrier on a strong ebb tide and in thick fog crashed into one of the gates and remained firmly stuck, demonstrating that navigational error or engine failure is still a risk and a hazard in providing adequate protection for London. The solution must almost certainly, sooner or later, rest with a new and higher permanent barrage incorporating a new well-tried lock system. There has been much talk about this but very little action. Meanwhile the authorities became increasingly interested in another ingenious interim solution.

The 'Flood Essex Policy'

This new, but in fact 3000-year-old, answer to the tidal flooding problem is not (so far as I know) on the official public agenda, but is known by every Thames Waterman I have spoken to as the **'Flood Essex Policy'.** Instead of closing all the sluices downriver in the event of a rogue surge-tide, all or some of them would be opened to divert the flood water over huge areas of low-lying land and abandoned industrial sites. If any residents and animals needed to be moved temporarily, they would have at least 6-12 hours notice thanks to the excellent warning system of tidal measuring stations now operating from the extreme North of Scotland down the East Coast and up the Thames Estuary. Coach and truck contractors on retainer contracts would be ready to provide ample emergency transport to designated temporary accommodation.

Up the East Coast it is possible to see how effective these measures can be. Between Burnham and Fambridge on the River Crouch, for example, the high sea-wall raised and strengthened after the 1953 flood was dynamited at intervals leaving large gaps through which the incoming tide can pour in and out harmlessly twice a day and now also provides adequate additional capacity to absorb freak surge-tides. Such a solution will help protect the town of Burnham on Crouch from the six-foot flooding it experienced in the High Street in 1953. The 'Flood Essex Policy' does, however, require investment within the flood zone in adequately walling round all installations, facilities and buildings requiring protection (see figure 1 overleaf) but it is a very cheap and simple interim alternative to the massive engineering and dredging projects previously on the drawing-board.

A New London Hub Airport

Second on our list of policy priorities is the opportunity opening up for a new London Hub Airport located in the Thames Estuary area. To fully understand why we give the airport such a high priority it is necessary to read not only what follows but also the final section of our conclusions.

Several sites for a large new hub airport have been suggested and put aside. Two remote sites to be reclaimed from wild water, swirling tides and constantly shifting sands were beyond Foulness Island on the Essex side and off the Isle of Sheppey. Both would have required immense dredging and earth-moving with long coffer-dams, high sea-walls and vulnerable connections with the mainland. Both were much further from London and exposed to icy, bleak winds and gales from the north through east. As a small-boat sailor for fifty years using these desolate and dangerous swatchways, I would not want to be out there arriving from the ends of the earth in extreme weather conditions or in the dense mist or fog that so frequently blankets that area and wondering whether we might over- or under-shoot the runway. I once spent a cold night of driving rain and snow in November out there hard aground on the Barrow Sand laying out anchors and warps to pull us free when the tide returned eight hours later. That was enough. Equally beating up the Spaniard Channels across the Kentish flats off Sheppey every year over a very uneven sea-bottom en route from Ramsgate to the Medway and on several occasions with a freshening south-westerly gale kicking up a very confused sea convinces me that this would be a very odd place indeed to locate a major international airport.

Within the last year, a much sounder alternative has come to the fore. Lord Foster of Foster and Partners who designed the new Chek Lap Kok Airport in Hong Kong proposes siting the new airport on the Isle of Grain on firm, dry, flat land just upriver to the west from the entrance to the River Medway. In terms of cost and connections, this makes a lot of sense with only short rail and road links to the M2, M20 and M25 motorways, to the Eurostar high-speed rail route and proposed new bridges and tunnels across the Estuary. Other fast links to Central London include the existing helicopter route up the River, dedicated fast catamarans, and feeder air services could assist with rapid transfers to and from Stansted, Southend, Manston (now Kent International), Gatwick and City airports. With the majority of flights landing most of the time across open sea from the East, there would be no bans on night-flights and only a very small fraction of the quarter of a million residents close to the Heathrow flight-paths currently complaining of significant noise intrusion would be affected. Indeed there would be strong commercial and economic interest in keeping the runways open round the clock.

The argument for a single new London international airport is that Heathrow is rapidly losing its premier hub status. It can handle 87 flights per hour from its two runways and its capacity use is said to be approaching 98%. By contrast, Paris Charles de Gaulle can handle 114 flights per hour from four runways; Amsterdam Schipol has six runways; Madrid four; Frankfurt four – all are aiming for close to 120 flights per hour by 2015. Already Heathrow is falling behind: it has direct flights to 157 destinations compared to 224 from Charles de Gaulle and 235 from Frankfurt. Even if Heathrow twins with Gatwick and is linked by a proposed 175 mph dedicated rail tunnel, the system will take at least five years for such a complicated project to be given the go-ahead and a further five to ten years to build. Even then the two airports need permission (so far withheld) to add new runways.

The new Isle of Grain London Airport would have a capacity of 150 million passengers per year, more than double Heathrow's present capacity, making

Fig 1: the blue shading and hatching on this map, drawn in November 2011, show the danger areas in the event of a tidal surge.

it certainly the largest international airport in the world. Foster and Partners in association with Halcrow engineering consultants believe they could have the airport up and running by 2030 given prompt and strong support from the government.

The Sewage Problem

Our third priority is the pressing problem of sewage. When, in October 2011, David Walliams completed his 215-mile charity swim from the source of the Thames to Westminster, it was reported that over 110 million imperial gallons (500,000 cubic metres) of raw sewage had entered the River in that short period of several days. Each year, say Thames Water, 40 million tons of raw sewage spills into the River untreated.

At least this is better than the Great Stench or Stink of 1858 when sittings in Parliament had to be suspended on account of the strong smells and there was very serious concern about a cholera epidemic, contamination of the drinking water and other health issues. The popularity of the new flushing lavatories was already causing havoc below ground. Happily the right person was on hand then at the right time, Joseph Bazalgette was appointed Chief Engineer to the Metropolitan Board of Works in 1855 and he set about building the system we have today. Within ten years he had constructed 83 miles of main sewers that discharged 400 million gallons per day into the Thames at Barking and Plumstead. That system, extended further downriver on both North and South Banks and equipped with extensive filtration plants and now power stations fed by the compressed solid waste, is now in need of massive overhaul, renovation and new relief sewers.

The solution currently under consideration is to construct a huge new main relief sewer for 20 miles (32 kilometres) running up to 250 feet (75 metres) below ground level and following the line of the River except at the Greenwich Peninsula where it would take a short cut under the Peninsula south of the O_2. The capacity of the pipe would be such that it could hold temporarily significant volumes of water coming down the River after heavy rains, an additional tool for flood prevention upriver. It might also be of value in conjunction with the operation of new surge-tide flood barriers or barrages downstream. The Great Sewer survey vessel is already hard at work on the River identifying the optimum route of the pipe.

Institutional Underpinning

Our 1972-75 LORICA meetings, publications and reports came to one very important conclusion. It was that the UK was then ill-equipped institutionally to co-ordinate long-term policy on the future of the London River. As to be expected, this struck some resonance at the time with the Greater London Council and the Port of London Authority. The fact of the matter is that this division and difference of interest persists but the gap between City Hall and the Mayor of London on the one side and the Port of London Authority and the shipping industry is closing fast under the strong leadership of City Hall.

The New London Gateway Port

The focus of the Port of London Authority is now very much directed to the disposal of the Tilbury Docks and to the new privately-owned deepwater London Gateway Port under construction at the old Shell Thames Haven refinery, storage and crude oil and product berths well beyond the River entrance and on the North Bank of the Estuary. This brand-new container facility is due to open in late-2013 and aims to handle 1.6 million containers in its first year and, once the huge logistics park is completed, to increase capacity to 3.5 million containers per year. This compares with the Port of Felixstowe's plans to expand from the current 3.5 million containers (40% of UK throughput today) to over five million. Felixstowe has just opened its first deepwater berths capable of accommodating the new generation of super-size container ships, each over a quarter of a mile in length and much wider and heavier than hitherto that will begin to enter service worldwide in 2013.

The Port of London Authority is likely to retain its responsibilities for navigation and ownership of the sea-bed along the full 95-mile (150 km) length of the tidal Thames, but its scope of interest and employment roll (360) may be increasingly skewed towards Tilbury and the Gateway. It will also be very concerned about the proposals to build a new super-airport on the opposite side of the Estuary and any interference this might mean with the navigation channels in and out of the London Gateway Port and the London River.

Other Important Issues

The experience of running the 2012 London Olympics in Stratford, Greenwich (equestrian events in the Royal Park), Woolwich (shooting) and at the North Greenwich (0_2) Arena on the Greenwich Peninsula will bring to the fore the immediate and long-term traffic, public transport and development challenges facing this part of London.

Greenwich and the London River are putting on a tremendous show through 2012 with celebrations covering the granting of Royal status to the Borough of Greenwich and other events. A river cavalcade with a thousand vessels will mark the 60th Jubilee anniversary of the reign of HM the Queen. A gathering and processions of 20 tall-ships in the Woolwich Reach and the arrival of many large vessels in the West India Dock will provide additional accommodation and national bases (such as the cruise ship Deutschland which will host the German teams) and bring much life to the Canary Wharf area, and many other celebrations and fireworks are planned for the Tower to Westminster sector of the River. Special events in Hyde Park and other parts of Central London are also planned.

It will be vital that the legacy of the 2012 Olympics is not merely the impetus it gives to sport of all kinds all over the United Kingdom, but also the kick-start it can give to economic growth and sensible investment in the longer-term prosperity and welfare of this country. In this, London and the London River and Londoners have an important part to play, not only in their own backyard but as part of a much wider national vision of regeneration and growth. At the end of the day, the challenge is not so much about national budget allocation or the regulation of the private sector. It is about the fundamentals of our society – freedom of the individual, human rights, protection of the weak and elderly, rising educational and employment

opportunity for all on equal terms, health care available to all, openness to
the rest of the world and a secure climate for investment in new technology
and new markets. This ideal only works if everyone and particularly every
institution involved understands this general long-term objective and abandons
the all too common conflicting instinct of seeking narrow, temporary and
sometimes random alliances to prevent things from happening.

Renewing Public Optimism

Greenwich, among many other places in the UK, is a good example of where
the achievement and dynamism of the past has been lovingly preserved and
protected for the benefit of inspiring future generations not merely with the
beauty of its buildings, park and riverside and the great historical treasures
they contain, but also with an awareness of the dynamism and wisdom and
artistry of the people who created them. This national pride and confidence
in the future has, of course, to be matched by an awareness that the world is
changing very fast indeed. Here lie great new opportunities for the United
Kingdom. The widespread global use of English, the City of London,
still the greatest financial market in the world, the opportunity to restore
London's position as the transport hub of Europe and top international airport
worldwide cannot be brushed aside. Global integration through advances in
telecommunications and the spread of global trade and markets give the UK
immense advantages, but only if they can be harnessed effectively.

Fundamental Objectives

Finally, with these wider and deeper preoccupations about the national psyche
and new opportunities within the global economic framework, I propose to
repeat an exercise we undertook with LORICA forty years ago. We asked five
questions:

- What might we hope to achieve over the next thirty or forty years on the
  London River?

- What are the long-term dangers and risks?

- What are the immediate priorities?

- What might be the key opportunities?

- How might an overall vision help in an efficient allocation of resources?

We cannot pretend to know how the future will work out. Others will have their own views, but neither will they know. All we can do is to apply our own grading of high probability to remote possibility and to look for savings and elimination of waste in the process. Most important is listening and observing the response of others to what we say, not merely the major players in the game today, but the scientists and engineers and commercial innovators at the edge of technological change.

A Forty-Year Horizon to 2052

Here is a list of what we might hope to achieve on the London River

•An abundant and constant supply of fresh clean water. This will involve close monitoring of the aquifers and tributaries of the Thames Basin, some new reservoirs and a radical overhaul of the distribution and sewage system resulting in zero spillage and a much cleaner River Thames.

•100% protection from freak tidal flooding, particularly the Central London area and new population concentrations such as Canary Wharf, Woolwich, Thamesmead, Tilbury, Gravesend and Southend. This will involve the completion of a much more secure new tidal barrage or barrier and comprehensive protection along the riverbank upriver and downriver.

•Intensive development behind these new defences, a new industrial and manufacturing hub dependent on very close links with Continental Europe and, hopefully, a large new international hub airport and container port located in the Estuary area. This should be just one part of a growth and investment strategy for the entire country.

Dangers and Risks

There are many dangers and risks ahead, but possibly the greatest is ending up doing nothing or next-to-nothing.

Let us focus, for example, on the risk of London sustaining massive damage from another freak tidal flood. The incidence of such tidal surges is roughly every 25 years over the last four hundred years, but many earlier floods were recorded. In 1242 in the Great Hall of Westminster "men did row with wherries in the midst of the Hall ... and took their horses because the water ran overall" while at Woolwich a great number of inhabitants were drowned and "at Lamberhithe, the Thames drowned houses and fields over a space of six miles". More recently, exceptional tides causing serious flooding occurred in 1791, 1834, 1852, 1874, 1875, 1881, 1928, 1953 and again, thanks to the new defences and higher river walls, without serious flooding, in 1978.

Today, we know that the danger starts on the Eastern Seaboard of USA and Canada, where the warm water of the Gulf Stream flows north to meet the icy Labrador current. In certain westerly conditions this results quite frequently in a wave typically about one foot in height and up to several hundred miles in length being generated that passes round the top of Scotland, where it can be easily measured, and into the North Sea. Normally it dissipates here, but occasionally if the weather changes, this water is driven south by strong north or north-easterly winds towards the Netherlands and our East Coast. Here the water-level rises much higher because of the funnel effect of the North Sea and the same phenomenon occurs on a much more dramatic scale at the entrance to the London River after the rogue surge-tide is compressed into a width of about half-a-mile. As Professor Hermann Bondi concluded half a century ago, there is no good reason to assume that this event will not happen again and over the last half-century, there is firm evidence that the wave-height and recorded tidal height could be increasing.

When the Barrier was formally opened in 1984, it was expected that full closure would be necessary for training purposes three times a year but not at all for other reasons. Between 1983 and 2010, however, the Barrier has been raised 119 times, of which 76 were to protect against tidal flooding and 43 to alleviate fluvial flooding after heavy rain in the Upper Thames Valley.

The flooding of Central London would inflict immense damage on the UK economy and that is why its prevention must remain top of the policy agenda.

Other Immediate Priorities

Second on the list of immediate priorities is the need to decide on the location of a new hub international airport with an annual capacity of 150 million, whether in the Thames Estuary area or elsewhere, and to press ahead as fast as possible.

Third is to forge ahead with the new relief sewer down the route of the river-bed and to modernise the existing distribution and sewage system at a much faster pace than hitherto.

Fourth is the construction of new reservoirs upriver to ensure the ample provision of clean fresh water.

Fifth is the construction of new river crossings including a new road tunnel connecting the Greenwich Peninsula to the Royal Docks and a new vehicle ferry between Beckton and Thamesmead.

New Opportunities: Wake Up, London!

The biggest new opportunity is to re-evaluate these five projects in the light of their impact on each other. There are immense savings to be made if the five projects can dovetail into each other. At present the custodians of each of the projects tend to present themselves as being in competition with each other for funds and government approval. If they were all five moving forward together simultaneously and cooperatively, a whole raft of new options opens up. There may indeed be opportunities for example for the Isle of Grain airport to generate its own tide-based electricity and for its design to be an integral part of surge-flood control. The exposure of the Medway conurbation to surge-tide flooding might be alleviated and the vast areas of the Medway and Swale River salt-marshes gradually recovered for development.

The Benefits of Co-ordination

If the location of the replacement barrier or barrage can be settled and the flow of the London River fully controlled, the superfluous shallows of the River, at present many square miles of unappealing mud at low tide, could be gradually walled off and sold off, piece by piece, for development, leisure use and new manufacturing and new industries. First, the Great Sewer project can consider the option of a much cheaper, more accessible and shallower route up the abandoned river-bed and its extension further downriver – just what Bazalgette achieved behind his new wall along the Victoria Embankment; there he found space not only for his North Bank sewer but what is now the District and Central Underground line. The possibility of new road or rail routes, or both, following the River - conventional, underground or overhead - would offer major relief to London's traffic problems. It could give the metropolis a new central artery and relief for the congested M25 ring-road motorway and the North and South Circular Roads. The cleansing of the River offers wide new opportunities for leisure use and amenities – new riverside parks, new marinas, dinghy, sailing and rowing clubs, new athletics centres and swimming-pools. Perhaps, in another forty years, our grandchildren and their children might even be launching new aquatic sports on the River and, unthinkable and at present vigorously discouraged on health grounds, possibly even river swimming clubs.

River Passenger Services

At the present, there is one spectacular success. We already have a splendid new fast river passenger service running frequently and reliably between Westminster and Woolwich. The authorities and operators deserve credit for this achievement.

What Could Happen to Old Father Thames?

Extracts from a feature article by the author in *The Times*, 8 August 1975

A Choice "Today, Londoners are faced with a choice. Should their own river be abandoned or not? For centuries, it has been the main artery of the capital; the docks were a focal point for trade; the shipyards, for industry; it was a highway for commerce and pageantry and a major outlet for leisure. Today the channels silt and the wharfage crumbles as the Port of London retreats towards the sea. But the opportunity now exists to make much more of the river..."

A Motorway? "The most radical solution would be to resolve London's traffic problems by doing away with the river as we know it. An 8- or 10-lane motorway up the river bed between dams at, say, Woolwich and Kew might obviate the need for more elaborate and more socially disruptive orbital and radial routes. The stream of traffic would bring life to this forgotten artery and its sunken character would protect the capital from undue noise and fumes. Many of the road and rail over- and under-passes for such a highway are, of course, already constructed and in use. In addition, the necessary new reservoirs and flood plains upriver would resolve London's water-supply problem and the dam downstream would protect Central London, once and for all, from the serious danger of tidal flooding..."

High-speed river transport "The major transport problem on either shore downstream from the City is the acute congestion on the main road and rail routes. Bottlenecks are frequent and savage. Journey times are slow and frustration intense. High-speed river transport, competitively-priced and intensely operated could provide considerable relief. Compared with road and rail improvements, the infrastructure costs in terms of new piers and car-parks are negligible. Commuter use of the craft in the morning and evening can also be linked with tourist services during the day..."

Secretary of the London River Commuters Association (LORICA)

The Future of the River

Extracts from *Downstream to Greenwich – The Heritage and Future of the London River* by Paul Tempest

Largely Derelict for a Decade

"While the whole River is 'a liquid 'istory', a historical goldmine for the antiquarian, few would argue that the stretch between Tower Bridge and Greenwich Pier has much of architectural merit...The square mile of the old Surrey Docks behind Cuckold's Point, an area as great as the City of London and within two miles from it, has been largely derelict for a decade. While some sections of the waterfront prosper, there are many more sections in ruins or where commercial activity has virtually ceased."

The People and Politics of the River

"The sturdy docker communities of Rotherhithe, Wapping, Deptford and the Isle of Dogs suffered intense war-time bombing, neglect in the period of post-war reconstruction and finally the transfer and transformation of their livelihood to the new cargo-handling facilities downstream. The remnant, still deeply rooted in the older terraces, splendid pubs and corner shops, are strong in the Borough Councils where they can scrutinise the more grandiose schemes for expensive yacht marinas, luxury private riverside residences and white-collar dormitories, but are unable to generate the compensatory impetus for public sector investment. The result appears, at first sight, to be political stalemate."

A Corner has been Turned

'The tidal river is, in fact, already becoming a much more attractive place. Thanks to the post-war Clean Air legislation and our changing weather pattern, far less of the soot and dust of the West End is dumped on the East

End than before. Both air and the river-water are cleaner: fish are returning to the river and the problems of effluents are under stricter control...Where 80,000 Thames Watermen worked, less than 1500 are left.'

A Hope for the Future

It may be that our children's children will look more to the River. As the energy cycle begins to project the economy along a new path, they might look back to the River of today and see it not so much in terms of commercial and industrial decline, but more as in transition to a new role, through which some of the best of our maritime, architectural and social heritage was stubbornly preserved. At least we might hope that our grandchildren will find by the River something of the bustling activity, visual excitement and quiet charm that our grandparents have enjoyed – and not just a derelict, stinking eyesore.

High Speed on the London River

Extracts from the illustrated paper by Paul Tempest commissioned and distributed widely by the Port of London Authority in 1978 and later included as an insert in the Port of London Authority monthly magazine.

High-speed Pipedreams

'Over the years, there have been many pipedreams, plans and projects to whisk travellers rapidly from the Thames Estuary and intermediate points into the Cities of London and Westminster. Monorails on stilts; river-line underground services; motorways over, in or under the river; diversions of the river into Middlesex and Surrey are only a few. Perhaps mercifully for all those who love the river, nearly all the grand ideas evaporated as soon as the accountants and bankers began to count the cost...'

A Notable Success and Several Failures

'From the first daily service by steam paddler – to Gravesend in 1815 – the popularity of the river as a valuable transport link and outlet for leisure grew steadily. One steamboat company's books for the year 1861 record 3,207,558 passengers landed at Old Shades Pier in the City, an average of over 10,000 per working day... but the steamers were no match in the long run for the fast new rail services springing up on both banks. The railway had reached Greenwich in 1838 and rapidly the commuters were weaned away from the river, leaving the paddlers to focus on day-trips and the new holiday trade. A valiant attempt in 1905 by the London County Council to take over the steamboat services and to run commuter services at cheap rates quickly ran into financial trouble: an election was fought and lost on the issue and the service abandoned. In 1951, prompted by the need to link the Festival of Britain site on the South Bank at Waterloo with the various piers on the North Bank and with the new Battersea Gardens Funfair, launched their waterbus service. Within a short time, the regular services were suspended.'

Lessons Learnt

Tourist use of the river fluctuated widely according to season and weather, but was much easier to satisfy than the requirements of regular commuters. Daily travellers would only switch back to the river if services were frequent, comfortable, reliable and as cheap or almost as cheap as the alternatives. But most important of all, the commuters required high-speed. For this they had to wait until 1972-76.

The Thames Love Song

Sung by sailors and entertainers widely up and down the River for centuries with endless variants to reflect personal and local needs, aspirations and occasions.

I met a girl on Tilbury strand
Beside the ferry standing
And oh, the love I felt for her
It passed my understanding

I took her sailing on the river
Flow sweet river, flow
London town was mine to give her
Sweet Thames flow softly

I combed the Graves End for a crown
Flow, sweet river, flow
And found a ring at Silver Town
Sweet Thames flow softly

At Dagenham I held her hand
At Blackwall Point I held her
At the Isle of Dogs I sweetly kissed her
And lovingly embraced her

From Greenwich pealed the wedding bells
As loudly they were ringing
I kissed her once again at Wapping
And all my heart was singing

But now alas the tide has turned
My love has gone far from me
And winter's frost has touched my heart
And put a chill upon me

Swift the Thames runs to the sea
Flow sweet river, flow
Bearing ships and parts of me
Sweet Thames flow softly

Andrea Jensen

Acknowledgements

I would like first to thank the various members of the London River Commuters Association (LORICA), founded in 1972. Over the last 40 years they have individually and collectively provided a strong input into thinking about the future of the Thames as well as a welcome stream of contributions and comment for our eight guide-books and pamphlets published, sold and distributed over that period.

A special thank-you goes to those who provided comments on the draft text of these books, notably Peter Kent, Tim Smith and Neil Macfadyen, and for their work on this book, Kitty Carruthers, Peter Harrigan and Samantha Elverson of Medina Publishing.

Paul Tempest
Greenwich, April 2012

Blackwall Tunnel 1897

Bibliography

Ackroyd, Peter, *Thames, Sacred River*, Chatto & Windus, 2007

Atterbury, Paul and Haines, Anthony, *The Thames*, Weidenfeld & Nicolson, 1998

Belloc, Hilaire, *The Historic Thames*, Hamish Hamilton, 1914

Eade, Brian, *Forgotten Thames*, Sutton Publishing, 2002

Hamilton, Olive and Nigel, *Royal Greenwich*, The Greenwich Bookshop, 1969

Harrison, Ian, *The Thames from Source to Sea*, Harper Collins, 2002

Howard, Philip, *London's River*, Hamish Hamilton, 1975

Johnson, Boris, *Johnsons' Life of London*, Harper Press, 2011

Kent, Peter, *The Guide (monthly)*, 1980-2010

Leapman, Michael, *London's River*, Pavilion Books, 1991

Pudney, John, *Crossing London's River – the bridges, ferries and tunnels crossing the Thames tideway in London*, J.M. Dent & Sons, 1972

Quiney, Anthony, *A Year in the Life of Greenwich Park*, Frances Lincoln, 2009

Tempest, Paul, *To Work by River*, GLC and LORICA, 1972

> *Downstream to Greenwich*, illustrated by Neil Macfadyen, sponsored by the GLC and introduced by its Chair, Dame Evelyn Denington. Conway Maritime Press, 1975

> *High Speed on the London River*, Port of London Authority, 1978

> *Gateway – The Future of the London River*, Teapot, London, 2001

Tempest Stephen, *Greenwich and Blackheath*, Teapot Press, London, 1989

> *Greenwich at the Millennium*, Teapot Press, London, 1999

Thurman, Christopher, *London's River*, Tempus Publishing, 2003

Photographs © Stephen Tempest with the exception of the following:

Bill Cannon p135(b); Kitty Carruthers cover flap, p3(t), p7(b); Getty Images front cover (b,3rd left), p2(t), p6; Rod Jones p41(l); KPMG Thames Clippers pp122-123; London 2012 pp11-12, p19; National Maritime Museum front cover (tr), p2 (b), pp26-27, pp104-5; Steve Tanner and Morgan Lowndes p70; (t); Paul Tyagi (Thinkfarm) p101(b);

medinapublishing.com